CW01521529

Your Music is Your Business

An insider's guide to writing hit songs and making money in the modern-day music industry

Jeff Topp

This book is dedicated to my two daughters, Jasmine and Amelie-Rose.

Contents

Foreword

OK, so if you are anything like me, you will sometimes listen to a song on the radio and think, "How did that become such a success? I could have done better than that." Or is it just me?

The art of song writing seemed like a taboo subject when I first dipped my toe in to that world. Something only for the selected few who had the fortune to pay their way, or know someone of influence, in the music industry.

I knew I could write good melodies and catchy hooks and even string some half meaningful lyrics together, but I was a long way from getting my music heard by the masses!

I also had the problem of not having a strong enough voice to be the front man and go out and perform my own smash hit songs (well. I thought they were pretty good tunes!). So, I was stuck in my own world with a bag full of ideas but no way of getting them out to my adoring fans (sorry, daydream time!). The only fans I had were my parents and my mate, Neil.

Neil was and still is a good mate and a huge lover of music. Oh, and a harsh critic! As a music lover, he presided as judge and jury when it came to my tunes, whether he knew about it or not. I always remember writing what I thought was a cracking riff-based catchy song only for Neil to say he didn't like it. Now, I am not one for dismissing songs so quickly, but to a degree Neil represented what the masses might have also felt if they had heard the track. Was Neil right or wrong? Well, that's the question that all songwriters should ask themselves when someone shoots their material down.

At the time I felt quite hurt about the fact that someone (my good mate) dismissed my song/s straight away, but overtime I began to realise that I should use his comments as constructive criticism and not take them to heart. As we all know, your music is very personal to you and it can be very hard to have your precious masterpieces torn apart.

This got me to start exploring the world of song writing in more detail. I was a hobby guitar player at heart and first I wanted to get a better knowledge of the instrument and learn new techniques. So, as a mature student, I enrolled myself on to a music diploma course at my nearest university in Brighton. Working full-time and completing a full-time diploma course isn't something for the fainthearted but it meant that my whole life for the time of the course was spent playing and understanding the world I now call my profession.

The tools, techniques, skills, industry knowledge and music theory I learnt from that one course and the experiences I had when I was studying with likeminded folk was so rewarding and enlightening. So, my song-writing journey started here!

Fast forward to now and I am a successful songwriter with a list of credits to my name. I have had songs played all over the world from TV and Film placements to radio play on commercial stations and even corporate videos for businesses. BUT I am not famous and not many people know who I am…and that's the way I like it.

So, to this book. If you are like me, someone who doesn't read a lot but wants to get to the nub of the facts quickly, then this is right up your street. I cover everything you need to become a successful songwriter and to make an income from your musical skill. Learn the basics of a song structure, melody, harmony, lyrics writing, and basic theory through to understanding how the industry works, what opportunities are out there for you, professional associations you must be a member of, and lots more besides. If you come across music terms that you don't understand, then don't worry, as there is a glossary at the back of the book listing some of the theory terminology you will come across.

Don't let anyone spoil your musical dreams. Learn, apply and enjoy your new career to come!

Happy song writing!

Jeff

Chapter One

Building Blocks for Song Structure.

Before we start, list three qualities that you look (or should I say, listen) for in the songs that you love. As writers, we sometimes don't listen to what's in our own head, as we are focused on wanting everyone else to like our songs. But we are listeners and customers too and we all know what styles, sounds and instruments we like to hear.

I'm a huge fan of the band James, a British group that has been making music for over 25 years. Not all their songs appeal to everyone but a few of their biggest hits, *Sit Down* and *She's a Star*, follow a classic song structure pattern, where some of their other not so well-known songs are more for the hardened fans. In other words, they produced the hits in the early years, which gained them their fan base, so everything else they produced after the fans would listen to and, of course, buy.

Simple really, we just need to produce the hit first. Easy! I hear you cry. If it was that easy, we would all be doing it!

So, what makes a potential listener like and then purchase your song?

While there's no real formula to crafting a potential hit, there are methodologies to it. As anyone who has spent time listening to lots of music can tell, hit songs come in a few well-defined forms. This is no accident. These writers, producers and singers all know how to put together a song that will probably be a smash. So how do you think the pros do it? They listen to hits of the past and they use them as resources for their ideas. That's one of the less well-kept secrets of pop song writing. The way they make it their own is by using some of the skills mentioned below to make variations.

OK, so what are the sections of a song? Now, I may be preaching to the educated here but it's good to recap the basics, as this is where many fail.

Typical sections

(Don't take this as a completed song structure as it would be a very short song!)

Intro – The introduction of your song. This is where you capture the listener's ear, either with a catchy riff or heavy drum opening. Again, no rules here but the catchier the better.

Verse – The storytelling section where you grab the listener by the hand and take them on your journey.

Pre-Chorus – Setting up of the chorus in a way of excitement and suspense. Imagine a pre-chorus to be like the moment you see that big box under the Christmas tree and realise it has your name on it!

Chorus – BOOM! The bit your adoring fans will be singing back at you. This is the highlight part of the song where you can put your catchy hook and lyrics together, producing what we call a cadence. (More about this later.)

Bridge / Middle 8 – This is where we can take the listener to another area or space in the song. Like a branch line to another mainline track. It also keeps the interest going as you can change the dynamics and direction of the song.

Solo – Instrumental solo normally but not exclusively. Most radio commercial songs won't have long solos as they like their songs to be short for their listeners' attention span. A good example of this is Thin Lizzy's *The Boys Are Back in Town*. The album-length version features the longer solo, but the radio version cuts the end solo short to get back to the catchy main riff.

Outro – Tidying up the loose ends either by repeating the intro or chorus but sometimes with a solid ending such as a drum fill, stab, holding a sustained chord, or even a fadeout.

The structure of a song will determine what kind of effect it will have on the listener, whether it will be a hit or not. One of the most common and possibly the most effective forms of a hit to write is the verse/chorus. This song form goes hand in hand with the dynamics of the audience:

1. The audience usually listens to the story the verses are telling.
2. And then the chorus will come around, summarising the story as the audience sings along.

Lyrically speaking, the chorus is going to summarise the main idea of the lyric and is going to be the emotional high point – the highest intensity section – of your song. It wouldn't be a bad idea to include the song title in there too. You want people to know what your song is called, right? Now, how do you want the music to feel? Want something happy and upbeat? Make your chorus major key with a high tempo and maybe use eighth notes. Want something a bit funkier and maybe a bit more intimate? Slow the tempo down and use a **mixolydian** mode instead.

What is Cadence?

OK, so let's imagine you are reading a great story that suddenly ends with no outcome! Well, that doesn't happen does it. Writers need a way of wrapping up a story to complete its journey: the end etc. The same can be applied to music. A cadence is a combination of chords that bring a section, a movement, or an entire piece of music to a close. A cadence is a definitive resolution to indicate that the piece is over. The end.

Once the general feel of the chorus is in place, we can start to think about emphasis. If you're featuring your title in the chorus, the **cadence** is going to be your friend. By having the title 'straddle' the **cadence** – starting at the beginning and then ending on the I chord – you're guaranteed to have it planted in the listener's head. Let's not forget the melodic tools we still have at our disposal. Long notes will make any lyric, especially the title, far more dramatic. Ending on the downbeat, on the first beat of the measure, is a subtle but a very common way to bring out the title too. What do *Message in a Bottle, No Woman No Cry* and *Born in the USA* all have in common? They were all massive hits, and they all used these melodic tools to their advantage.

Any hit needs to be greater than the sum of its parts and the section that is going to make up most of those parts is the verses. As the verse is a supporting idea, many successful tracks will have verses that remain melodically, harmonically and lyrically static. This ensures that your verses don't pull the power away from other sections. For example, the same way that we use cadences to ramp up the chorus, we shouldn't be using cadences in the verses.

Instead, you could resolve to have your verses end on chords that aren't the **tonic**.

I mentioned before that you're going to be telling the story in the verses. If you want to build a conversational vibe in the verses, make use of short notes, a limited pitch range, and having the melody in the low to middle register. All of this doesn't mean that the lyrics need to be boring. The audience is going to be listening during the verses. That means that the verses can be the perfect time to bring in some complex, sophisticated melodic ideas.

You may need two more sections to act as connective tissue for the verses and the chorus: the bridge and the pre-chorus. These sections function in similar ways and can connect and contrast with the material that comes before and after, and they both build intensity into the next section.

Lyrically speaking, our bridge will contrast in content with the verse and the chorus. This can be as simple as changing the tense, by generalising if the lyrics prior were specific, or by focusing on a new emotion. Musically speaking, you can make the bridge 'move' with a different chord progression, then the verse or chorus (and again, avoiding a cadence), or by having the bridge modulate away and back to the key of the song. Making the bridge a bar longer or shorter than the other sections is a great way to build tension.

The pre-chorus will also contrast with the chorus and verse melodically, harmonically and formally. However, a pre-chorus will also break down the intensity at the beginning of the section only to ratchet it back up towards the end into the coming chorus. Slowing things down, lower notes and longer phrases will break the intensity down. To build the pre-chorus back up near the end, an ascending melodic shape and losing some of the space between the words will get the audience ready for the chorus.

Within a single type of song form, the verse / chorus, there are endless possibilities and countless variations to be made. Let's explore some other forms and variations.

Form

Form, by the way, is the musical term for the structure.

There are as many different songs as there are songwriters, but modern popular song writing, including folk, blues, pop and rock songs, build upon basic types of songs or 'songs form'. Understanding the basic song forms and their traditions helps the songwriter decide upon the appropriate structure for the type of songs they want to write. Song forms can be broadly divided into the **stanzaic** and **non-stanzaic**, or elaborate forms, that use the assigned letters A, B and C and the AAA form.

Stanzaic Songs

According to Charles Hartman of Connecticut College in the US, **strophic**, or **stanzaic**, songs have a single unit, called a strophe or stanza, that is repeated an indefinite number of times. Stanzaic songs are strongly associated with the folk music tradition. The ballad stanza consists of four lines in which the first and third beats are four beats long and the second and fourth lines three beats long. The first line can also be shortened to three beats. The second and fourth lines rhyme, and sometimes the first and third lines rhyme as well. The classic 12-bar blues song uses rhymed stanzas of three lines in which the second line repeats the first. According the book *Money Chords*, the third line of the 12-bar blues song is the answer phrase, which musically and lyrically answers the statement of the first two lines, as in the example from *Outlaw Blues* by Bob Dylan: *"Ain't it hard to stumble when you've got no place to fall?"* (twice), answered by *"In this whole wide world I've got nothing at all."*

Verse-and-Chorus Songs

Stanzaic songs may include a refrain at the end of the stanza. Long and complex refrains are found in songs with a verse-and-chorus structure. When the words and music of the chorus are the same each time, but the verses have the same music with different words each time, the song has an extended refrain. Most popular songs from the classic rock period are written in the verse-and-chorus form, which has been around since the mid-19th century. A common type of verse-and-chorus song uses 8-bar verses and choruses, as in The Beatles' *Get Back* and Journey's *Don't Stop Believing*.

Elaborate Non-Stanzaic Forms

Songs with verses and choruses strain the definition of a stanzaic song because they alternate between the different units of verse and chorus. Elaborate versions of non-strophic songs are associated with Tin Pan Alley and show-tune song writing, and the structures of these types of songs are assigned a letter. Commonly, the assigned letters are A for verses, B for choruses and C for the bridge. The most common non-stanzaic song structure is AABA, with The Beatles *I Want to Hold Your Hand* as one of thousands of examples. From the perspective of this type of song writing structure, the stanzaic song form is AAA,

16

which is the oldest song form and is associated with folk music.

- AABA

The AABA format was the predominant song writing format in popular music in the first half of the 20th century. Songs in the AABA format consist of four sections, each eight bars long. The A section is the main section of the song - the verse - and it repeats the most often. The B section, also referred to as the bridge or middle 8, represents a change in mood in the song by often presenting contrasting lyrics and chords. This song writing format was popularised by Tin Pan Alley, a collective of various songwriters and publishers in New York City, where song writing greats like Irving Berlin and George Gershwin worked. The AABA format died out in the 1960s with the popularity of rock & roll and the rise of groups like The Beatles. Before The Beatles broke off into other song writing formats, they utilised the AABA format in songs such as *From Me to You* and *Do You Want to Know a Secret*?

- AB

The verse-chorus format has been the song writing format of choice for modern popular music since the 1960s. Unlike the AABA format, which highlights the verse, the verse-chorus format puts emphasis on the chorus. In this form, verse serves as a build up to the chorus, which has the major hook and catchiest part of the song. Verse-chorus songs sometimes include a bridge, but it usually only appears once, if at all. You can hear the verse-chorus format in a variety of songs, spanning genres, from The Police's *Every Little Thing She Does is Magic* to Britney Spears' *Oops, I Did It Again*. The format is so prevalent that Kurt Cobain, who used the format often, almost named a song *Verse Chorus Verse*.

- AAB

The 12-bar form in the AAB pattern is synonymous with the blues. Most blues songs are in the AAB format. Like the AABA format, the AAB form doesn't have a definitive chorus. The major hook of the song, in which the title most often appears, is in the B section. The AAB form utilises what are referred to as the I-IV-V chords. (Check out the theory section for more detail on this.)

The A section starts on the I chord and consists of a set of lyrics sung over four bars. The second A section repeats itself but starts on the IV chord. The B section begins on the V chord and consists of a different lyric, usually a response to the A section, which resolves back on the I chord of the A section. *Dust My Broom* by Elmore James is just one example of the AAB format.

OK, before we go on, we do need to mention *The Great American Songbook*. You may have heard of it and thought it was a songbook that you could buy from a good music shop. I did initially! Well, that's not really the case. *The Great American Songbook* was and still is the canon of the most important and influential American popular songs and jazz standards from the early 20th century. Many of these songs use the AABA form. It includes the most popular and enduring songs from the 1920s to the 1950s that were created for Broadway theatre, musical theatre and Hollywood musical film. The music of this genre is also often referred to as 'American standards'.

The times in which much of this music was written were tumultuous ones for a rapidly growing and changing America. The music of *The Great American Songbook* offered hope of better days during the Great Depression, built morale during two world wars, helped build social bridges within the culture, and whistled beside us during unprecedented economic growth.

The Great American Songbook genre has emerged within the last hundred years, so there is no real consensus on exactly what falls under its heading. Several scholars have completed significant research into the genre and have helped to shape the definition of *The Great American Songbook*. Alec Wilder's *American Popular Song: The Great Innovators, 1900–1950*, lists and ranks the artists he

19

believes belong to *The Great American Songbook* canon. Wilder suggests that *The Great American Songbook* era ended in 1950; others maintain that its end coincided with the dramatic increase in the popularity of rock & roll music in the late 1950s and early 1960s, and some still believe it lives on to this day.

Sections in Detail

Let's take a look at the individual parts of our song form in more detail.

The Verse

In the dramatic context of musical theatre, where most of *The Great American Songbook* originated, the verse became a transitional section leading us from dialogue and action into the more artificial world of song and dance. It works like an intro or set-up for the song proper, and typically has a free musical structure, speech-like rhythms and **rubato** delivery.

The Pre-chorus

The pre-chorus is a particular style of bridge. Designed with specific intent of lifting the level of intensity up and into the climax of a final triumphant pop-chorus - an emotional effect achieved through the use of musical devices like harmony, tempo, melody, instrumentation, arrangement and production; sometimes something as simple and effective as a **change of key**.

- It's called a pre-chorus because it precedes the chorus.
- It's called a climb because it rises towards a higher level of emotion.
- It's called a build because it increases the intensity.
- It's called a rise or a lift for the same reasons.

The Chorus

The chorus is the element of the song that repeats at least once, both musically and lyrically. It is almost always of greater musical and emotional intensity than the verse. The chorus, which gets its name from a usual thickening of texture from the addition of backing vocals, is always a discrete section that usually prolongs the tonic and carries an unvaried poetic text. In terms of narrative, the chorus conveys the main message or theme of the song. It usually contains the hook and is normally the most memorable element of the song for listeners. In the modern formula, the chorus becomes the main course, the central core of the song, and the primary focus of the composer's creativity and inventiveness.

The Pop-chorus

Like the modern chorus of the previous era, the pop-chorus is the central focus of the song. Unlike its predecessor, however, it eschews the more complex sophistications of structure in favour of a straight return to the single distinctive repeated and repeatable strophic sections, at least eight bars in length, but containing an essential ability to repeat a hook with high frequency inside the standard three or four minutes of a pop song. The successful pop-chorus expresses a song's core identity.

The Hook

This is a relatively recent concept. It is a musical idea used to catch the listener's ear and hook their attention. As such, we have to admit it's certainly not a completely new thing. I mean, even old dead classical music guys used phrases and figures intentionally to do the same. And surely the simpler folk-forms worked that way, too. What is relatively recent is that it has been given a special new name and elevated to a major principle in pop.

You have to have a hook. The hook is 'what you're selling', a recognition of pop's commercial imperative. The hook is your tagline for the song. It could be a motif like Keith Richards' dirty guitar riff on *Satisfaction* or the theremin melody, which opens the Beach Boys' *Good Vibration*. It can equally be the title, like the shout out and join in *We Are the Champions* from Queen, or some other key lyric line or image. As often as not, the hook will be found right there in the pop-chorus. And sometimes the hook *is* the chorus - as in Springsteen's *Born in the USA*. It can be anything in any place and in any fashion, you choose - just as long as it happens. And whatever it is, it will happen more than merely once or twice.

The Bridge/ Middle 8

The term Bridge or Middle 8 in pop usage seems to have been completely severed from its roots in the standard 32-bar AABA chorus and is now applied much more casually to describe pretty much any linking passage between one section and another. It's a looser and less specific use of the term than before but has the advantage of being readily understood as an identifier for a separate and intervening section of song, which is neither verse nor chorus.

With all of the above in mind, if you are keen to work in the commercial music world, then you will have to squeeze everything within four minutes.

So why fewer than four minutes and why do we have guidelines for the length? As it turns out, average hit song length has more to do with historical limitation than an audience's focus level. Let's take a quick trip back in time to the beginning of the record. In the early 1900s, the most common way to release music was via a 10-inch record. The 10" usually played at a speed of 78 revolutions per minute (rpm), which measures the frequency of a rotation.

Early 10" records could only hold three to five minutes per side. 12-inch records were also used, but they only held about four to five minutes. If it went longer than that, the grooves became too close together...the sound quality went down, thus, musicians in the first half of the 20th century were artistically bound by technological constraints. The limitation meant pop artists had to create quick tracks that fit the mould if they wanted a song to be released as a single. A short single could be played on the radio and become a hit song.

In those days, if you recorded a song that was longer than three minutes and 15 seconds, they just wouldn't play it.

Naturally, there were exceptions, but they were reserved for other genres. Duke Ellington could record longer songs because jazz had different rules.

In the pop world, exceptions were rare and relied on deception. One example of a song breaking the 3:15-minute rule was the 1964 smash, *"You've Lost That Lovin' Feelin'* by The Righteous Brothers.

Produced and co-penned by hit maker Phil Spector, the song was actually 3:45 minutes, much longer than its contemporaries. Unwilling to cut it down, Spector stamped 3:05 minutes on the single, so DJs would play it without realising its actual length.

It went on to become the most played song of the 20th century on American radio and television.

Chapter Two

10-Step Process to Song Writing

We all need a destination in our lives to head for! And the same goes for our songs. As songwriters, we are constantly looking for great song material. We're also looking to express our ideas with an artistic voice that is as unique as we are. Furthermore, most of us want to simplify the process and expand our marketability.

One important key to marketability in the hit song market is, of course, content. Effective songs paint rich images for the listener. Imagine that your songs are paintings. Are you the proud creator of stick figures scrawled across construction paper, or does your palette of texture, colour and light capture the desires and deepest wanderings of those gazing upon it? To ensure that the latter is the case, you can use a writing process called destination writing. In destination writing, we begin with one key word—a place—as the momentum for your song content.

The key to destination writing is to use all of your senses—touch, taste, smell, sight, sound, and also movement—as springboards for creativity. When those senses are involved, the writing springs to life. The connection that your audience makes with your lyrics

26

depends on the power of this one key word. But how do we build that connection with the audience? By illustrating our piece through specifics and actions.

We immediately know the meanings of words like 'walk' and 'say'. But these words are generic and will not engage an audience by themselves. But there are dynamic alternatives. Consider the sentence below:

Instead of: *And I was saying*

We could write*: We know what's being said, but it doesn't mean anything*

Or

Instead of: *And I was stuttering,*

We could write: *My mind knew the words, but I just couldn't be heard*

Both of these phrases swapped out the boring 'say' with verbs that are emotionally charged. Verbs and adjectives like these will keep your audience's attention. Once you've got a handle on which words will draw your audience, it is time to craft a compelling narrative. Any destination writing will consist of two types of detail: external and internal.

External and Internal

Assume that your song is centred on a primary character. The external details will be what is happening around your character and the internal details will be their thoughts and feelings. Any good song will have a mix of both. The art of combining internal and external detail is integral to providing balance in your lyrics. Too much internal detail and your song will be weighed down by the thoughts of the characters. Too much external and the audience will have nothing personal to identify with. So how are our words going to work with the music?

How we expect the melody to move is going to influence how the lyrics move as well. Every new melodic idea presented in a song – a movement from the verse to the pre-chorus, for example – will go hand in hand with a new lyrical idea. I'm sure you're familiar with *Mary Had a Little Lamb*.

Mary had a little lamb,
Whose fleece was white as snow,
Everywhere that Mary went,
The lamb was sure to go.

These fours lines contain two musical phrases (Mary had... white as snow) and two lyrical phrases (Everywhere...lamb was sure to go.). But this isn't the only way to attack these four lines. We could have kept describing the various attributes of Mary's little lamb over all four lines. In that case, we would continue the same melodic idea for the entire verse. We could also change ideas with each new line if we have a new melodic idea to accompany each.

The melodic phrasing determines not only where the topics begin and end but also where a rhyme might occur. In *Mary Had a Little Lamb*, the rhyme occurs between the two large musical phrases: 'Mary had a little lamb, whose fleece was white as snow' (Section A) and 'Everywhere that Mary went, the lamb was sure to go' (A). If the four lines were all representing four smaller melodic phrases, the rhyme scheme might look more like this. Note that wherever the melodic phrase closes, rhyme occurs.

Mary had a little lamb (A)

and Mary had a pony too (B)

the sun was rising on the land (A)

and May was slipping into June (B)

Once you have your primary lyrical sections in place and developed, it is time to contrast.

Imagine if every section of a song had the same number of lines, the same rhyme scheme, the same rhythm and the same toggling pattern. Sounds boring. By changing up the rhyme scheme, changing the rhythm, adding or subtracting lines, and altering the toggling pattern, a songwriter can keep things interesting over the course of their work.

As you can see, it's clear that the process of commercial song writing is based on a number of patterns. These patterns make up the content of hit songs and are patterns that a songwriter can reproduce while still maintaining a unique voice. Knowing these patterns is critical to the success of both beginners and experienced writers. The best way I've found to approach commercial song writing is through what is called the "**The 10-Step Process**."

Now there are many different lists like this in the music world but to me, this one covers everything you need. Use it as a reference/checklist every time you write. You don't have to use or include everything on the list, but it will help to focus your mind when and if it wanders.

The 10-Step Process

Step 1:
Destination-write.

Step 2:
Find rhyme pairs.

Step 3:
Choose a rhyme scheme and toggling
pattern.

Step 4:
Add prepositions and conjunctions.

Step 5:
Choose a plot progression.

Step 6:
Destination-write again using thought/feeling
language.

Step 7:
Look for titles and write the chorus.

Step 8:
Write a second verse and pre-chorus.

Step 9:
Write the bridge.

Step 10:
Assess verbs, tense, and point of view, and
conversational quality.

Steps in detail:

1.   Destination-write: we mentioned this at the beginning of this chapter. It's good to have a goal or story end to work towards. Some storywriters actually work out an ending of a story first and work back to the start. I like this process personally, otherwise to me it's like trying to start a painting and looking at a blank canvas and not knowing how to start. But you may find it easier yourself to work from start to end.

2/3.   Finding rhythm pairs and schemes are an extremely useful idea. I sometimes use a call and response rhythm pattern. i.e., my first rhythm/melody is setting up a phrase and then the second rhythm/melody is responding to my first. If you look back at *Mary Had a Little Lamb*, you can see how the first line and the second line 'Whose fleece was white as snow' are slightly different but still sound close enough to suggest that the rhythm works well together.

4.   Prepositions and Conjunctions. OK, this will take a bit of explaining but I will make it as user friendly as possible.

Prepositions:

In English, we use prepositions to connect nouns or between nouns and pronouns. Imagine that you encounter two nouns: *car* and *book*. You can use prepositions in many ways to connect the two nouns to express different ideas:

The book **about** the car

The book **by** the car

The book **behind** the car

The book **in front** *of* the car

The book **near** the car

The book **under** the car

The words in bold relate two nouns to each other. These relationship words are called prepositions.

Prepositions may be defined as any word or group of words that relate a noun or a pronoun to another word in the sentence. Prepositions never work alone; they're always with an object. In the earlier examples, the object of each preposition is *car.* Just to get all the annoying terminology over with at once, a prepositional phrase consists of a preposition and an object. The object of a preposition is always a noun or a pronoun, or perhaps one or two of each.

Conjunction

A conjunction is the glue that holds words, phrases and clauses (both dependent and independent) together. There are three different kinds of conjunctions, but we are going to look at two of them, coordinating and correlative. Each serves its own, distinct purpose, but all work to bring words together.

Coordinating conjunctions are what come to most people's minds when they hear the word "conjunction."

They can join together words, phrases and independent clauses. There are seven of them, and they're easy to remember if you can just recall **FANBOYS**:

- **F**or - explains reason or purpose (just like "because")
  *I go to the park every Sunday, **for** I love to feed the ducks on the lake.*
- **A**nd – adds one thing to another
  *I go to the park every Sunday to feed the ducks **and** watch the cricket.*
- **N**or - used to present an alternative negative idea to an already stated negative idea.
  *I don't go for the fresh air **nor** really for the ducks. Honestly, I just like the cricket.*
- **B**ut - shows contrast
  *The cricket in the park is entertaining in the spring, **but** it's better in the heat of summer.*
- **O**r - presents an alternative or a choice
  *The men play in teams: reds **or** blues.*
- **Y**et - introduces a contrasting idea that follows the preceding idea logically (similar to "but")
  *I always take a book to read, **yet** I never seem to turn a single page.*
- **S**o - indicates effect, result or consequence
  *I've started to take an interest cricket, **so** now I have a good excuse to watch the game each week and get some fresh air.*

Correlative conjunctions are sort of like tag-team conjunctions. They come in pairs, and you have to use both of them in different places in a sentence to make them work. They include pairs like both/and, whether/or, either/or, neither/nor, not/but and not only/but also.

- I **either** want the cheesecake **or** the brownie.
- I'll have **both** the cheesecake **and** the brownie.
- I didn't know **whether** you'd want the cheesecake **or** the brownie, so I got you both.
- Oh, you want **neither** the cheesecake **nor** the brownie. No problem.
- I'll eat them both - **not only** the cheesecake **but also** the brownie.
- I see you're in the mood **not** for dessert **but** for appetizers. I'll help you with those too.

5.   Plot: the plot is simply the dot to dots of your song. You need a plot to a) keep your listener engaged and b) to keep the focus and make sure you are on track to reach your end goal. A song without a plot or story line will end up just being a flaky piece of work that won't hold up against your peer's songs.

6.   More destination writing, but now with more thought about the feeling and emotional elements you

want to portray. How would this song affect you if you were listening to it? I always try (and I do mean try) to step out of the song writing process and listen back to either a rough recording or demo of what I have done. By doing this, you start to listen as a third party. This can become a cathartic process as you start to self-critique your work. BUT don't be too harsh and don't try and find fault if there isn't any. I have had moments where I have really liked some of my songs, to the point of playing them on loop in the car. If they are good, they are good!! Remember what I said at the beginning of the book, you are also a listener and buyer of music, so you know what works and what doesn't.

7/8.   You will need a title eventually. Most but not all songs feature the title within the song itself. It's normally found in the chorus, so if you have written your chorus lyrics already then you may have the title. To be honest, in my opinion the title doesn't serve as important as the song itself. If the song isn't very good, then the title is irrelevant. Also, consider the option of a pre-chorus. Pre-choruses bridge the gap between the verse and the main chorus. It's also a good tool to tie up the verse story to get ready to hit the next passage of your song.

9.   As explained earlier, the bridge can take your song on a tangent to give it a change of direction before coming

back to the powerhouse last chorus. A bridge, or as it's sometimes known, a Middle 8 (because it normally features over eight bars of music), is a good time to change the dynamics and key of the song. A key change is a great way to build excitement and energy to the climax of your song. If you listen to boy bands, such as Take That and Westlife, some of their biggest hits feature **tone up** key changes. I equate this as the moment they go from sitting on stools to getting up and moving forward. Trust me, we have all seen this and it can be witnessed on YouTube if you want to check it out! But in all seriousness, this is a very good weapon to your song armoury. An example of this is *You Raise Me Up,* originally sung by Brian Kennedy but covered by many different artists. You can hear how the song becomes uplifting and powerful by the way the key change comes in. If you are not sure of how a key change works, then check out the theory section of this book. It will revolutionise your song writing style.

10.   Really this is the final checkpoint for you. By now you should have your plot, goal and general form of your song sorted. You just need to make sure you have a credible storyline that without the music would stand up as a story in its own right.

By utilising all of these steps, you'll be able to craft commercially viable songs with ease.

Chapter Three

Harmony

Harmony is one of music's profound dimensions. It is a background player, supporting the rest of the sonic cast. While melody articulates the conscious narrative, harmony gives shape to a song's subconscious emotional message or subtext. From building suspense to lending your song a polished and balanced feel, without harmony, no other part of the song will have context.

When we're talking about harmony, we're often thinking about the groove. So, what is the groove? It's not just a funky bassline. The groove is a combination of elements—including tempo, feel and rhythm—that make up the rhythmic core of a song. Whether the groove is played by a lone guitarist or a 15-piece orchestra, all of these elements are present in their groove.

Individual groove elements are often very simple when heard out of context. The power of a song's harmony will come from how these simple elements work against each other and how they are developed. Visualise the sound of a lone sustained chord. Without a groove, that chord would hold only limited interest. However, inside a groove, that same chord could be interesting enough to last the duration of an entire song. There are endless rhythmic variations that can be used to build up a groove. A guitarist and a bass player might use the same rhythmic ideas, though the idea might be offset by a beat or two. Similarly, the rhythmic ideas of the groove may share rhythmic ideas in the melody. Basing some song's elements on others is an easy way to develop an organic, connected feel.

We can see how rhythm can add to the feel of the track. But how do we develop the overall sound? Like any artist, you have access to a palette of different colours to work with. Major, minor, power and seventh chords are four types of chordal colours. Each key colour can serve as a source for harmonies that will work with the primary chord. Let's describe a C major chord colour as bright yellow. Like a painter, you may choose to 'paint' your song entirely with that shade of yellow. However, as the emotions of a song become more subtle, you may find yourself wanting to use other shades of yellow, and maybe even related colours. These chord colours are suggestive too.

It's important to remember that harmony thrives on variation. Changing the progression's length, chord rhythm and chord order can all keep a harmony fresh. All of these are variations of timing, and the chords themselves, stay intact. Varying the timing and order of a chord progression preserves much of its essential character, and helps you adapt a standard progression to a song. These changes can highlight a unique lyric, change the pacing of the groove, build excitement, and otherwise support the songwriter's dramatic intentions.

Putting together these variations in timing, colour and rhythm are easy enough out of context. The real trick is putting everything together. But how do we develop the harmony throughout a song? Think back to some of the songs you've heard over the years. Many of these songs use the same chord progressions; chord progressions that become familiar very quickly. These progressions occur so often and are so powerful that I refer to them as power progressions. They are so strong, that you can use any one of them alone to suggest an entire key colour. The power progressions will be your constant allies as a songwriter. Consider the power progression below.

I   IV   V (1, 4 and 5 sequence)

This progression is arguably the most famous chord progression in rock music. Countless songs have been written around it. So, what can we do with it? What if the chord progressed backwards? How would it change the feel of the harmony by adding a minor second or a minor third into the progression? By simply considering the different chords we can add to this progression, we've opened up a Pandora's box.

But we are not just limited to the realm of major and minor. Let's look at how we can utilise **modes** in our progressions. For example, the difference between the major and **mixolydian** key colour is only one note. But what a difference it makes! Listen to Jimi Hendrix's *Manic Depression* and pay attention to the riff. The song moves in a I♭V II IV progression, another power progression. What kind of feel does it give the whole track? How does it support the lyrics? More importantly, now that you've heard it, what kind of variations could be made to mix things up a bit?

Power progressions like these are common phrases of speech, or expressions—tried and true musical objects. Though they may have been used countless times before, there is always something new that power progressions can be used to say. By modifying the power progressions, or any chord progressions, you can create endless variations of them, and spin countless songs from the same essential material.

Chord progressions, the power of a groove and the colours of the keys are all just barely scratching the surface of harmony. Harmony is the bedrock, the backbone of any song. Every harmonic development and every means of variation will become a tool in your arsenal. And the more harmonic tools you have at your disposal, the easier the song writing process will be.

You can refer to Chapter Six, *Song Writing Theory Made Easy. Ish!* if you are unsure of some of the musical terms above.

Chapter Four

Making Melody Work

Got a little tune in your head that needs to get out? Melody is one of the most important and immediate aspects of a song. It's the element that the audience sings along with. And that most intimately brings out the emotion of the lyric story. The melody also exists alongside and on top of the harmony. But that relationship can differ, depending on the effect you are trying to achieve with your song.

When we're setting our lyrics together with the melody, there are three considerations we need to make.

- What is the length of each note?
- What is the length of the phrases?
- What is the space between the phrases?

These may seem like trivial questions, but the note length, phrase length and phrase space will determine how your lyrics feel to the listener. Let's start with the notes. If you listen to Bob Marley's *No Woman, No Cry*, you'll find that the verses—which are conversational in tone and build the story of the track—generally have shorter notes. The chorus, where the title of the track is repeated, consists of longer notes. This is no accident. When lyrics are set to longer notes, they are emphasised and are automatically more dramatic.

The melodic phrases you use for your lyric sections can be of a standard or surprising length. Standard two and four bar phrases will give a song a steady feel. Surprising phrases – any other bar length – will keep things fresh and draw the listeners' attention. Good songs will have a mixture of both. And those phrases will gain additional power from the spaces in between them. Verses will benefit from having lyrics more closely packed together with little room to breathe. Choruses, on the other hand, benefit from being drawn out and require more space between the lyrics as a result. Once you have the basic lyrical ideas in place for your melody, try developing them with some repetition or present new ideas as a contrast.

Sure, setting the lyrics to your melody is important but it is the interaction between melody and harmony that will define your song. Let's say we already have a harmony in place, or we have a way in mind that we want our melody to work so we're not thinking of melodic ideas with no context. So, let's develop a pitch. When it comes to the pitch of a melody, there are three approaches.

1. Melody on Chords—where the melody stays on a chord.
2. Melody Over Chords—where the melody is in the key, but is only loosely related to the chords.
3. Melody Against a Bass Line (Counterpoint)—where there are two melodies and the vocal melody moves against a bass melody.

No matter what approach you take, you're going to start on one of the tones in the chord. Starting from the tones will allow you to build a compelling melody consisting of even the simplest materials and development. The example that comes to mind is Billy Joel's *We Didn't Start the Fire,* a song whose melody would resemble a straight line if mapped out. If you want to decorate a melodic line like this (and you might, considering how flat it could sound), you can zig-zag between the neighbouring notes that reside right above and below your original tone. However many chord tones you try to base your melody on, understand that each will have an effect, creating a distinct melodic shape.

- Stationary—a straight line
- Zig-zag—decorates a straight line with a neighbour
- Ascending—starts low and goes up
- Descending—starts high and goes down
- Arch—starts low, goes up and then down

- Inverted Arch—starts high, goes down and then back up

But say you really want to spice things up with your melody. Counterpoint between a bass line melody moving against the vocal melody might do the trick. But not all bass lines are built equal. The easiest way to determine if the bass melody would make for good counterpoint is if it could be sung. Bass lines that move all over the staff will be useless unless you're going to be scat singing.

There are four kinds of standard counterpoint: parallel, similar, oblique and contrary. If a bass line has the same melodic shape as the vocal line, then it is a form of parallel counterpoint. Similar counterpoint features a bass line and vocal melody that move in essentially the same direction, though not as closely as parallel.

Now here's where things get interesting; oblique counterpoint has either the bass or vocal line revolving around a limited number of notes. The bass line might stay on one note or move around in an **ostinato**. The vocal line will stay in basically the same place. If you've heard the opening verse of Led Zeppelin's *Stairway to Heaven,* then you've heard oblique counterpoint.

Finally, contrary counterpoint, as its name implies, has the bass and vocal lines moving in opposite directions; the bass line swings down while the vocal ascends, or vice versa.

Now, those of you who have written songs for years will probably have used the above methods without really thinking the categories they sit in. But it is a good idea to remember that there is always method behind everything we do in music. It also makes you look and sound cool if you know what you are trying to achieve!

The simplest methods of developing melody are tools you'll be using for the rest of your song-writing career.

Putting chords to your melody.

There are several things you can do to help you put a chord progression to an existing melody and they will make your life a lot easier. Here are a few of them:

- The first thing you should try to do is work out what key the melody is in. This will make it a lot easier, as if you know what key you're playing in, you can pick chords from that key. If you're not sure how to do this then check out my light bulb theory section in chapter six.

- Try putting a simple bass line to the melody. As bass lines are fairly easy to write, you should have no problem with this. Once you've got the bass line, take the root notes and use the chords that they correspond to. See if it fits.

- Try putting a standard chord progression to the melody. For example, I, IV, I, V. (In the key of C this would be C, F, C, G.) The reason this might work is that due to the way our Western musical ears are tuned, we automatically follow certain musical patterns without even thinking about it, subconsciously creating melodies that fit in with the 'norm.

- Strip the melody down to its bare essentials. Take out all the notes that aren't totally necessary to the overall feel of the melody and see if that makes it easier once you've got down to the core of the melody.

Here is an example of how I'd put chords to a melody. Let's start with a melody that everybody knows, *Amazing Grace*:

(If you don't know your musical notes on a music stave, there is a guide at the back of the book.)

Amazing Grace:

Traditional

Well, it's in the key of C major for a start as there are no **sharps** or **flats** in the **key signature**.

The notes in the second bar are C and E. So, it's in C major, the first accented note is a C and the notes in the bar are a C and an E, which are the root and third of the C major chord. Do you think a C chord might work here? Let's try it... OK, that works!

Next bar. The notes are an E and a D. The E lasts for the majority of the bar, however, so let's concentrate on that note. We'll try an E minor as it's the obvious choice, but if you play it, it doesn't sound very good so let's discard that chord. A minor (Am) also has an E in it, so let's try that chord. Much nicer, so we'll stick with that!

The next bar contains a C and an A so Am could work again here, but I have a hunch that we should go back to C. OK, that works well.

Where did my hunch come from? I thought it was an appropriate place to change the chord, and we'd just been on Am so I assumed that C would work. And as the main note in the bar is a C, it stood to reason that it would fit.

Next bar only contains the note G. As the chord G is in our key, and it seems obvious, let's try it. . . Bingo! It works.

The next bar is the same as the second bar, so I think it's safe to try a C there.

Next bar again is the same as the third so we'll stick an Am in there and it works a treat.

The next TWO bars seem to stay on G, so let's try a G chord holding it for two bars. Do you think that worked? Yes, it did, so it seems we have a chord progression here that's working. If we play the second half of the song using exactly the same chords, it works fine.

The only difference is the last two bars where we need to finish up with two bars of C major, instead of two bars of G major.

So, what guidelines did this melody follow?

- We ascertained the key as C major.
- All the notes were in the key, which made it easy. No accidental sharps or flats.
- The first AND last chords were C major, so it followed that basic rule.
- All the chords were within the key.
- By taking the main notes of the melody, we were able to attribute chords to them pretty easily.

And hopefully you learnt the following:

- How to take a basic melody and break it down, bar by bar, to find out what chords would fit.
- Different methods of working out the chords within a melody.
- How to ascertain the key a melody is being played in.

But hold on, if I made that look easy then it's because I know my basic theory. I was never one for theory when I first picked up the guitar, I just wanted to play the darn thing. The theory came later to me after realising that to advance my career in the industry, I would need to learn the dreaded music THEORY! So, I promise that when you get to the theory section, I will walk you through as I was taught it. Some of you will understand theory and be able to sight read well, but when it comes to song writing skills, the theory you need isn't just the ability to read music but to understand how to get the best from it. Music is maths, so if you like maths then you are on to a winner. If not, then you will get to learn not just music but math skills as well. Double winner!

Chapter Five

My Song Writing Process.

It is one thing talking and teaching about song writing but it is another putting it in to practice.

As well as writing songs from scratch with the hope of them making the commercial grade, I sometimes get commissions to produce songs in a certain style or for specific products. This makes life much easier as it gives me a reference and topic to start from. Now, if someone had told me many years ago that they would be paying me to write and do something I love, I would have laughed at them. So, if you are new to this then just remember we have all been there and anything is possible. You can do this.

I personally always start with the music, as I feel more comfortable with setting a bed for the lyrics. I'm lucky, as I tend to get melodies coming into my head sometimes without trying. I know this isn't the case for every songwriter and I know some really struggle with the melody but find lyric writing easy.

When I have my melody, musical phrase or even a hook, I don't worry about structure at this point as this is the fun, creative part of developing the song. It's good sometimes to just jam through ideas on your own. I normally record my ideas as I go along and then sometimes play along with that recording. I find this helps me a) to see if things are working musically and b) to see if I can introduce some harmony or counter melodies to the tune.

Chorus or verse first? Well, I actually like to try and get the catchy hook / chorus down first which means I'm a work backwards type of guy! By doing this I actually find it easier to write the verses musically and lyrically. Again, this is my way of doing it, you may have your own way and whatever works for you is important to you and your style. Song writing is an art form not a process that is set in stone.

From here I ask the following questions: Where is this song going? Who's the audience? Who is it for? Will it be for commercial or corporate use?

Every commission or project is different. Don't laugh, but I once had to write a song for a baby signing company who wanted to have a song that would be played at their music classes. You will see later in the book why you should take every opportunity that comes your way! I actually found this hard as at the time I didn't have any children or even close relatives who had kids I could use to help me understand what I needed to do.

So, I went to one of their classes to see it in action. I always recommend if you do get commissioned to write a song, go and find out about the subject. Then at least you can write knowing that you actually know what you are talking about. One thing was very clear from the class; the song had to be simple, repetitive and catchy. We were talking AAA form song writing here. Just to recap AAA is basically Verse, Verse and Verse but with variations within each one to create choruses.

The lyrics also had to be simple, short and not cluttered, as the teachers in the class would be signing to my song. All these factors had to be considered to develop a meaningful song.

So back to the questions, where is my song being pitched at, what audience, etc?! For arguments sake, let's say it's destined for the commercial world. My next move would then be to piece my already catchy hook chorus to a verse and see where we go from there. By now I may have already got lyrics for my chorus but nothing yet for my verse. No problem, as we can come back to those later. I like to get the music down and the form of the song structured before spending time on lyric writing. To me, the music is so important and, in my humble opinion, is the crux of the song itself.

So, now I have a chorus and a verse, I might consider slipping in a pre-chorus, but this might depend on the length of my chorus, or even verse. What I don't want is to overload the verse and pre-chorus to the extent of spending too much time on it. Remember, most attention spans are short, and people get bored easily. As mentioned earlier, most hit songs feature the chorus within the first minute so as not to lose the attention of the listener. I think this is a good tip to remember, especially for the commercial world. If you are writing for an album, then it's not so important.

Next, I might see about adding a bridge or even solo. This again acts as a good juxtaposition to add another element to your song. By now I might be up to about 2:30 to 2:50 in duration. This is the perfect spot to pop your bridge in, as it will give you just enough time to get back to your catchy chorus/outro before you hit the 4-minute mark. Which is actually too long for a commercial song. They like it to come between 3:20 to 3:50 if possible.

56

OK, so I have the bones of a track. I'll start working with lyrics and using the destination writing skill. Lyrics have never come easy to me as I tend to over think. What I do find works for me is to write every word or a short sentence that relates to my subject. For example, I recently wrote a song that was about losing a loved one. Not very cheerful I know, but 'sad songs say so much', according to Elton John. Writing an emotional song is quite tough because you tend to reflect on your own sadness in life, which isn't easy at times. So, for this I took words like void, pain, loss and hide, and these acted as my lyric building blocks. From there I created a few rhyming sentences using those words to come up with the following:

The love I have lost
The pain inside
Just creates a void
I just can't hide

You notice I have made lines two and four rhyme. This is a common technique in lyric writing.

Once I have worked out how the lyrics will fit with the music, then I start to work on developing the dynamics, timbre and harmony a bit more. I might start to look at some musical gems, which I call 'fireworks' within a song.

This is a part of the song that just sounds cool, such as when a vocal harmony comes in to play on a chorus, or the hint of a guitar solo under a verse to suggest where the song will go next.

These ideas come with experience, but you will know when it happens. When I hear a piece of music that features a 'firework' moment, it tends to make the hairs on the back of my neck stand up. Remember, music is a powerful tool that can play havoc with your emotions, so if you can make magic moments within your songs, they will appeal to the listener.

OK, so I now have a complete structure of the song and plenty of ideas for the lyrical content. The real test for me is to come back to it another day. By doing this it forces you to return to the project with fresh ears. Many times in the past I have written songs that I simply don't like the sound of when I revisit. Trust your musical instinct on this. BUT I do advise caution, as yes, it's good to be critical with your work but don't too critical to the point of hating everything you write, as that won't get you anywhere!

If you remember at the beginning of the book, I mentioned my mate Neil who was the 'main man' when it came to critiquing my work. Although I listened with trepidation to what he thought, I always took his points as constructive criticism, not negative. So, if you have someone who can be your critic, I'd advise you ask them to give you pros and cons of your song. If there are no cons, then great. Ask them to take the song away for a day, listen to it a few times and then get back to you. If there are still no cons, then the chances are your song will stand as a credible song.

If they come back and say 'I like it, but…' then don't take it to heart, just take on board their thoughts. Remember, you are the song writer who has worked so hard to learn your craft, you know what works and what doesn't and it's just by having a third party listen that will make you think outside of your song writing bubble.

Chapter Six

Song writing theory made easy. Ish!

Before we start, I'd like to point out that the word "theory" used to send shivers down my spine and never really interested me at all. So, let's start looking at theory as the building blocks to successful song writing and not the dusty topic we might remember from school. I also want to point out that you do NOT need to be able to read music. Some of you will know this already, I know, but many well-known musicians don't and can't sight-read. But let's start with why it's really important to have at least some grasp on the basics.

To begin with, music is a language. Take this paragraph, for instance. It's made up of sentences, which are made up of words, which are groups of letters. The letters are taken from the alphabet.

Music has an alphabet too, but we call it a scale. Each note is like a letter. We put notes from the scale together to make chords (words). Then we put the chords (words) together to make phrases (musical sentences.) Once you know how to make phrases sound good, you are well on your way to writing songs.

So, chords are your vocabulary. You need to know chords. But knowing chords alone is not enough. That would be like speaking words and not being able to make sentences. You need to know how chords flow from one to another.

Major scale:

There are many scales, but there is one that everyone needs to know and is the holy grail of Western modern music. The major scale.

The major scale has a particular sound. You've heard this sound many times before and you've probably sung it too:

Do, Re, Mi, Fa, So, La, Ti, Do.

That's it, that's the major scale.

Next, we simplify it. Instead of "Do, Re, Mi, Fa, So, La, Ti, Do," we use 1, 2, 3, 4, 5, 6, 7, then back to 1.

To show you how this relates to our musical notes, we are going to use the key of C which uses all the white keys on a piano. The black keys are the flat (♭) and sharp (♯) keys and they don't feature in a C major scale.

1	2	3	4	5	6	7	(8)
C	D	E	F	G	A	B	C
Do	Re	Mi	Fa	So	La	Ti	Do

The above are all the notes that feature in the key of C. When we get to the 8th note, then we start again. All the notes make up what we call an octave (8 notes).

At this point, you might think we should learn more about scales, and someday I hope you do. But to be honest, mastering the usage of the major scale will get you to understand how scales work and how they can be applied to every key.

It might be a surprise to some of you, but it's possible to write a very good song without knowing a lot about scales. When you play a chord, you can immediately hum several notes that seem to fit. This process of playing and singing while searching for a strong melody is automatic. You "hear" the vocal lines in your head, or you experiment until you discover something you like. Part of the fun of writing songs is this searching process. But while you can get along fine "discovering" the tune, it's a lot more useful to not take everything to chance and know your way around scales and how chords fit with melody. For that purpose, this is very useful.

Roman Numerals

Each note in the scale can be considered the starting point, or root, for a chord. In other words, there is a note we will call 1, and there is a chord made up of several notes, which uses note 1 as a starting point. Don't worry right now where those other notes come from. Just remember, there is a note called 1, and there is a chord based on note 1.

This chord based on note 1 is called the one chord, and we use a roman numeral one (I) when we are referring to this chord. So, if we want to talk about just the note, we will use 1, but if we're talking about the chord, we write I.

So, lets add this to our C major key:

I	ii	iii	IV	V	vi	vii	I
1	2	3	4	5	6	7	(8)
C	D	E	F	G	A	B	C

Do Re Mi Fa So La Ti Do

Some of the roman numerals are capitalised - I, IV, and V- while others are lower case - ii, iii, and vi - and this is intentional. The capitalised chords have a certain sound, which some people describe as happy or bright. In music theory, we call them major chords. The lower case chords have a sound some people hear as being darker or sad. We call these minor chords.

OK, why are these notes used in C when there are other notes available to us on our instrument? This is where we apply a bit of maths and produce a formula. As I mentioned earlier, music to me is like simple maths; if you get the maths right, then the music process is easy, well, easier to understand.

Tones and semitones

If we look at a keyboard, our notes are laid out in black and white and go from low (left of the keyboard) to high (right of the keyboard). If we were to play all the notes from left to right in succession, then this is called playing chromatically. On a guitar, for example, the notes (i.e., frets) are next to each other. So, if we start from the nut of the guitar (furthest part away from your body) and play every fret until you reach the body of the guitar, then again, we will be playing chromatically.

A semitone is the distance from one note to the next note chromatically. So, for example, if we play an E note, the next semitone note will be the F note. If you were to find this on a keyboard, you would see that there is no black note between the E and the F note. If we were to play a G note followed by the next semitone up, this would lead us to playing the G♯ (black) note.

A tone is basically two semitones away. So, if you were to play a C note and then play a tone up from there, your next note would be a D. In other words, you jump over the C♯ note.

Back to our major scale and let's see how tones and semitones feature within the C scale.

T	T	S/T	T	T	T	S/T	
1	2	3	4	5	6	7	(8)
C	D	E	F	G	A	B	C

C to D is a tone (T)
D to E is a tone (T)
E to F is a semitone (S/T)
F to G is a tone (T)
G to A is a tone (T)
A to B is a tone (T)
B to C is a semitone (S/T)

Now we start to see a pattern form for our major scale. In fact, this is what we call the formula of a major scale

$$T, T, S/T, T, T, T, S/T$$

So, we have had a look at the key of C. What about other keys? Well, we use the same formula to work out every key. Let's look at G, which is quite a popular key for guitarists as the chords are pretty easy for the novice player.

If we apply the major scale formula to the G scale, then we get the following notes.

T	T	S/T	T	T	T	S/T	
1	**2**	**3**	**4**	**5**	**6**	**7**	**(8)**
G	**A**	**B**	**C**	**D**	**E**	**F♯**	**G**

Can you see that we now have the note of F♯ in the scale? Because we have started on a different note, this has taken us on a different path to include the F♯. If you want to try this on a keyboard, then it might be a good way to help understand the formula better.

Major Scales Chart

Scale	1	2	3	4	5	6	7
C♭ Major	C♭	D♭	E♭	F♭	G♭	A♭	B♭
G♭ Major	G♭	A♭	B♭	C♭	D♭	E♭	F
D♭ Major	D♭	E♭	F	G♭	A♭	B♭	C
A♭ Major	A♭	B♭	C	D♭	E♭	F	G
E♭ Major	E♭	F	G	A♭	B♭	C	D
B♭ Major	B♭	C	D	E♭	F	G	A
F Major	F	G	A	B♭	C	D	E
C Major	C	D	E	F	G	A	B
G Major	G	A	B	C	D	E	F♯
D Major	D	E	F♯	G	A	B	C♯
A Major	A	B	C♯	D	E	F♯	G♯
E Major	E	F♯	G♯	A	B	C♯	D♯
B Major	B	C♯	D♯	E	F♯	G♯	A♯
F♯ Major	F#	G#	A#	B	C#	D#	E#
C♯ Major	C#	D#	E#	F#	G#	A#	B#

Right, we now know which notes feature in each key, but what use is that unless we know how to use the scales to build the correct chords and chord sequences? So, next we need to harmonise the scale, or to give it its proper term, diatonic harmony. What is this? I hear you ask. Well, it's a fancy word that describes the way of saying chords or notes related to a certain key. Every scale has a collection of chords that fit it perfectly because these chords are built from the notes within the chosen scale. When this was first explained to me, a light bulb went on in my brain and suddenly song writing became so much clearer.

Let's go back to our C major scale (remember the major scale is the gospel in Western/modern music). We need to work out which chords to use if we are in the key of C, and by using another formula we can do that.

1	2	3	4	5	6	7	(8)
C	D	E	F	G	A	B	C

We need to work out the chords first. If we take the 1st, 3rd and 5th notes of the C scale, it gives us C – E – G. If we play these notes together, then we have played the C major chord. Try it out on your instrument!

Next, we take the 2nd note of the scale (D), 4th note (F) and 6th (A). Can you see that all we are doing is taking a note and leapfrogging the next and then repeating it again? If we put D – F – A together, it produces a D minor chord.

If you do that with every note in the scale, you end up with this:

1	2	3	4	5	6	7	8
C	D	E	F	G	A	B	C

C + E + G	=	C major	I
D + F + A	=	D minor	ii
E + G + B	=	E minor	iii
F + A + C	=	F major	IV
G + B + D	=	G major	V
A + C + E	=	A minor	vi
B + D + F	=	B diminished	vii

So, there you have it. All the main chords in the C major scale. If you notice on the right, you have the roman numerals shown for each chord. We sometimes use numerals as opposed to numbers when writing out chord charts. More on that later.

To recap: what you can see here is technically called harmonising a scale, whereby you take the 1st, 3rd and 5th, then 2nd, 4th and 6th, then 3rd, 5th and 7th notes etc, to produce the chords. When you go past 7, then you start at the beginning again.

Chord Inversions

Suppose you are playing a simple D chord. You look down at your hand and notice you are playing three notes: D, an F♯, and an A. You ask, "What would happen if I let go of the D note and replaced it with another D further up the keyboard/fretboard?" You would still have a D chord, but it would be a different arrangement of the three notes. The idea here is that as long as you are playing a D, an F♯, and an A, regardless of where they are located on the instrument, you are playing a D chord.

Slash Chords

Until now, every time we play a D chord, the bass note is always a D. What would happen if we played the F♯ or the A instead? We would still be playing a D chord but changing the bass note makes a big difference. It makes such a big difference that we have a way of indicating when we want the bass note to be one of those other possibilities. We call them slash chords.

When we want a D chord with D in the bass, we write D. When we want the F♯ in the bass, we write D/F♯. When we want the A in the bass, we write D/A.

Seventh Chord / Dominant 7th

The seventh chords have in common that the seventh note in a scale is added to a triad (a three-note chord), making it a four-note chord

The name "dominant" refers to the fifth degree of the diatonic scale and it is called dominant because it is most weighty besides the tonic (the root of the scale). The most common dominant chord is a dominant seventh, in which a minor seventh is added to a triad major. A less common alternative chord name for C7 is Cdom7 (dom stands for dominant). The seventh chord belongs also to the group of extended chords. Note that the fifth sometimes are omitted when these chords are inverted. A slight dissonance could be heard in 7th chords because one of the notes, the seventh, is not included in the same key as the root note.

Major 7th

Major 7th is constructed by adding the seventh tone in the scale to a major triad.

Minor 7th

Minor 7th is constructed by adding a minor seventh tone in the scale to a minor triad. Similar to the 7th chord, a slight dissonance could be heard in minor 7th chords because one of the notes, the seventh, is not included in the same key as the root note.

Let's just have a look at common 7th chords in the key of C major:

C maj7th   C   E   G   (B)   B is the 7th note of the C scale

C min7th   C   Eb   G   (B♭)   E and B are both flattened by a semitone

C7   C   E   G   (B♭)   Only B is flattened by a semitone

The Circle of Fifths

Suppose we take the 15 written major keys and put them in a straight line, beginning with 7 flats on the far left, moving towards C (no sharps or flats) and then continuing to 7 sharps on the far right...

7♭, 6♭, 5♭, 4♭, 3♭, 2♭, 1♭, 0, 1♯, 2♯, 3♯, 4♯, 5♯, 6♯, 7♯
The names of the keys would be...

C♭, G♭, D♭, A♭, E♭, ♭♭, F, C, G, D, A, E, B, F♯, C♯

Then imagine we wrapped this straight line around a clock with C at the top. (Because there are 15 keys represented on the line, and only 12 places on the clock, there will be a little bit of overlap at the bottom.) The resulting figure is called the Circle of Fifths. In music theory, we call the interval from C to G a fifth, because G is the fifth note in the C major scale. D is the fifth note in the G major scale, and so on around the circle.

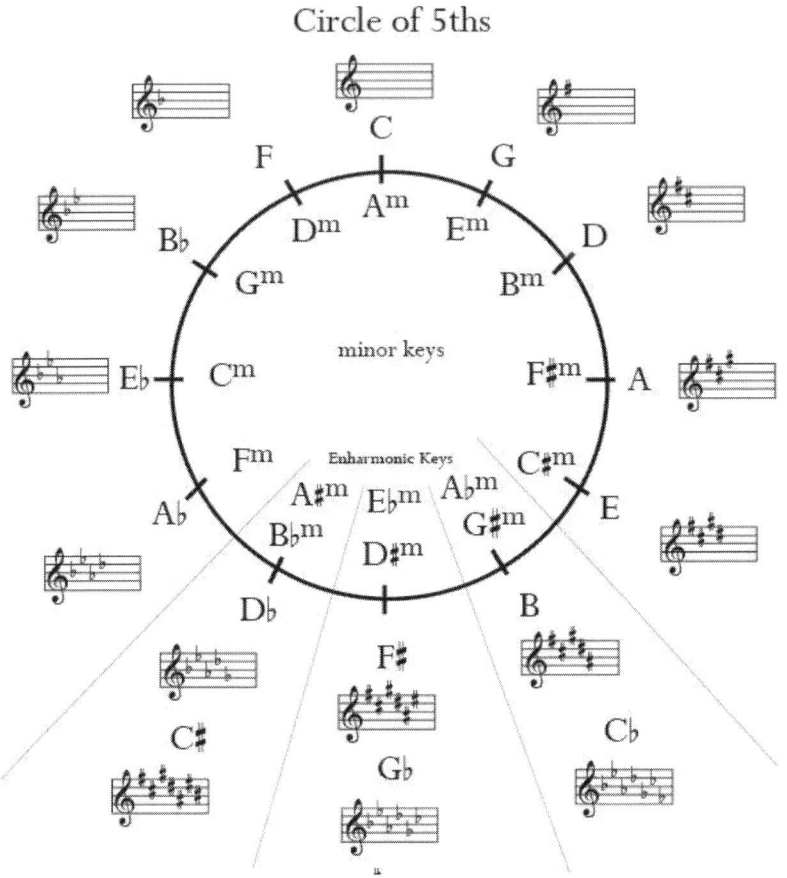

The inner circle of chords are the minor keys associated with the correct major keys. (i.e., Am is the relative minor for the key of C.)

An interesting thing about the circle is that it's possible to write songs that use part or all of the circle as the progression. For example, you could start with a C chord, move to F, follow that with B♭, and keep going until you get back to C. Also, if you need to work out a classic 12 bar blues (I, IV and V) sequence, then take any note as the root (I) chord, then go to the next note left of your root note and this will give you the (IV) chord. Then go to the note right of the root note and this will give you the (V) chord. Try it, as it's a very useful way to learn your chord sequences.

Understanding Modes

Ok, strap in and hold on tight! I think explaining about modes is harder than demonstrating. We will be using a keyboard to explain the mode process, so if you have a piano/keyboard to hand, then it might be worth trying it as you read further.

Imagine for a moment that time rolled backwards, and you found yourself in a chapter in history where they had not yet discovered the sharps and flats. Pianos (which wouldn't have been around yet, but if they had been...) were only white notes, and the only major scale available was C.

So, you accepted those limitations and wrote a few songs in the key of C major. But then you wanted a new sound, something different... so you looked down at your hands, and the thought came through, "What if I shifted my hands one note to the right?"

Let me pause here to correct a possible misinterpretation. In our modern world of music, we have a concept called transposing. By that we mean that we can take a song and move every note up (or down) by a certain number of tones and semitones. When we do this, the result is a little higher (or lower), but because we shifted every note the same amount, the song still sounds like it did before. The relative jumps from note to note have not changed.

Now back to our unusual piano missing the black notes... We know that the jumps from note to note in the C major scale follow the formula tone – tone –semitone –tone – tone – tone - semitone. In other words, the distance from note 1 to note 2 is a wider gap than from 3 to 4. So even though our unusual piano may look to our eyes as though each note is evenly spaced, we know in the world of sound and frequencies it isn't that way. Perhaps an easier way of saying it is... just because the black notes have not yet been discovered doesn't mean they are not there. We still have to leave a space for them in our minds, because we know they are going to come along later.

You shifted your hands one note to the right and played one of the songs you had written in C major, but now, because you had shifted it, and because the whole and half step jumps are at a different place under your hands, this new version of your song sounded quite different.

Great! We wanted a different sound. That was the purpose of shifting the song in the first place. So far, so good.

So, then you stepped back for a minute and asked, "What was it I just did?" And then you realise that you took the original key of C major (where we number the notes 1, 2, 3, 4, 5, 6, 7 - with the note C being note 1, D being note 2, and so on), and renumbered it so the D is now note 1, E is note 2, etc.

Then you realised there was nothing to stop you from shifting again. What if E was note 1, or F, or G? In fact, there are seven different notes, any one of which could be note 1. Therefore, you could play your song in seven different places, the original (in C major) and six other versions... by shifting the song to the right.

When this becomes clear in your thinking, there's something else important to grasp. We used the key of C major in our example because it's easy to see that all the notes are evenly spaced, and you can imagine shifting your hands one note to the right without any difficulty. But stepping back into the present, we could have used any of the 12 major keys on our modern piano.

For example, the key of D♭ major has five black notes and two white notes. Keep those seven notes and remove the rest. Now five white notes are missing. It's not as easy this time to play the same song while shifting (because the scale notes, being both black and white, are not spaced evenly). Still, with practice you could probably do it. And you could renumber the notes just like we did before... the maths isn't any harder. What this means is that any song (using only scale notes) written in any of the 12 major keys can be played in its original location (where note 1 is the name of the key), and can also be played six other ways, each time shifting the hands one more scale note to the right, and renumbering the keys so that note 1 is at a new place.

This idea of shifting the song needed some names, and so the ancient Greeks (because they were thinking about this) gave each shift a name.

IONIAN
Played in the original major scale.

DORIAN
Played one scale note to the right. (The original note 2 is now note 1.)

PHRYGIAN
Played two scale notes to the right. (The original note 3 is now note 1.)

LYDIAN
Played three scale notes to the right. (The original note 4 is now note 1.)

MIXOLYDIAN
Played four scale notes to the right. (The original note 5 is now note 1.)

AEOLIAN
Played five scale notes to the right. (The original note 6 is now note 1.)

LOCRIAN
Played six scale notes to the right. (The original note 7 is now note 1.)

To think this through and understand what's happening, first you need to know the major scale we looked at earlier and you also have to know that Ionian mode is associated with note 1 of the major scale, Dorian with 2, Phrygian with 3, Lydian with 4, Mixolydian with 5, Aeolian with 6, and Locrian with 7. Knowing these two things, you can then work through an example.

Let's take A Dorian as our example. We know that Dorian is built on note 2 of the major scale. Which major scale has A as note 2? The answer is G. The G major scale is the place where we will find A Dorian as one of the possible shifts. So far, so good.

Now, what about the scale? We remember the G major scale starts on note G and climbs through the notes A, B, C, D, E and then instead of playing note F, we play F♯. So, the G major scale is G, A, B, C, D, E, F♯, G. Also, these notes are numbered in our minds. G is 1, A is 2, and so on up to F♯, which is 7.

To play A Dorian, we play the same notes, but now A is 1, B is 2, all the way up to G, which is now 7. So, the scale is A, B, C, D, E, F♯, G, A.

Next, which chords are available? Again, we use what we already know about G major. The basic chords found in G major are G, Am, Bm, C, D, and Em (and there is one more... the vii chord, which is F♯ diminished. You may include this chord if you like, but you'll probably find yourself using the first six chords a lot and the vii chord less often).

Because we are in Dorian, the Am chord is now the "home" chord, and the other chords are available to use in progressions.

Some progressions would come to you right away; Am-G-Am, or Am-Em-Am, or Am-C-D-Am. In a short time, you would discover quite a few more. These are your building blocks for writing songs in A Dorian.

You might wonder, "Do I need a big map for A Dorian?" The answer is no. Remember, there are five notes missing from each octave of the piano, so chords which might have used those extra five notes are not available. This knocks out a lot of possibilities. Playing just the six chords (or seven if you use the vii chord) keeps you in the mode.

The last question is a little more involved. Suppose you are playing an instrument, perhaps an instrument that plays just one note at a time, and you don't want to associate A Dorian with the G major scale, because that takes a long time to think about. In fact, as soon as you hear the name A, you picture the A scale. So, you would rather hear the word Dorian as indicating a change to be made to the A major scale. So somehow, we've got to get to the A Dorian scale beginning with the picture for the A major scale. To do this we compare the A Dorian scale

(A, B, C, D, E, F♯, G)

to the A major scale

(A, B, C♯, D, E, F♯, G♯)

Notice the differences are in notes 3 and 7. Both are down a semitone in the Dorian version. So, we could make a rule to memorise. We'll use X as a variable, as in maths, to stand for any note on our modern keyboard. Here's the rule - "To play X Dorian, play the X major scale with notes 3 and 7 down a semitone."

The Rules

This idea of memorising rules can be applied to the other modes as well. We'll add the rules to what we already know. As before, X can represent any note.

IONIAN
Played in the original major scale.

DORIAN

Played one scale note to the right. (The original note 2 is now note 1.) Or another way of thinking about it... X Dorian - play the X major scale with notes 3 and 7 down a semitone. To remember this rule, picture the D major scale. Notice that notes 3 and 7 need to be lowered to lose all the sharps and flats.

PHRYGIAN

Played two scale notes to the right. (The original note 3 is now note 1.) Or another way of thinking about it... X Phrygian - play the X major scale with notes 2, 3, 6 and 7 down a semitone. To remember this rule, picture the E major scale. Notice that notes 2, 3, 6 and 7 need to be lowered to lose all the sharps and flats.

LYDIAN

Played three scale notes to the right. (The original note 4 is now note 1.) Or another way of thinking about it... X Lydian - play the X major scale with note 4 raised a semitone. To remember this rule, picture the F major scale. Notice that note 4 needs to be raised to lose all the sharps and flats.

MIXOLYDIAN

Played four scale notes to the right. (The original note 5 is now note 1.) Or another way of thinking about it... X Mixolydian - play the X major scale with note 7 down a semitone. To remember this rule, picture the G major scale. Notice that note 4 needs to be lowered to lose all the sharps and flats.

AEOLIAN

Played five scale notes to the right. (The original note 6 is now note 1.) Or another way of thinking about it... X Aeolian - play the X major scale with notes 3, 6 and 7 down a semitone. To remember this rule, picture the A major scale. Notice that notes 3, 6 and 7 need to be lowered to lose all the sharps and flats.

LOCRIAN

Played six scale notes to the right. (The original note 7 is now note 1.) Or another way of thinking about it... X Locrian - play the X major scale with notes 2, 3, 5, 6 and 7 down a semitone. To remember this rule, picture the B major scale. Notice that notes 2, 3, 5, 6 and 7 need to be lowered to lose all the sharps and flats.

Chords In All Major Keys

Major Keys	I	ii	iii	IV	V	vi	vii°
C	C	Dm	Em	F	G	Am	B°
C#	C#	D#m	E#m	F#	G#	A#m	B#°
D♭	D♭	E♭m	Fm	G♭	A♭	B♭m	C°
D	D	Em	F#m	G	A	Bm	C#°
E♭	E♭	Fm	Gm	A♭	B♭	Cm	D°
E	E	F#m	G#m	A	B	C#m	D#°
F	F	Gm	Am	B♭	C	Dm	E°
F#	F#	G#m	A#m	B	C#	D#m	E#°
G♭	G♭	A♭m	B♭m	C♭	D♭	E♭m	F°
G	G	Am	Bm	C	D	Em	F#°
A♭	A♭	B♭m	Cm	D♭	E♭	Fm	G°
A	A	Bm	C#m	D	E	F#m	G#°
B♭	B♭	Cm	Dm	E♭	F	Gm	A°
B	B	C#m	D#m	E	F#	G#m	A#°

The chord chart above lists all the common triads belonging to each key.
Roman numerals indicate each chord's position relative to the scale.

Music theory isn't for everyone and it may take some time to put the theory in to practice, but knowing just a small amount of music theory can really open up your song writing skills and bring another dimension and depth to your material.

Chapter Seven

Know Your Music Business

Right, let's get down to the important stuff. Knowledge is a lot of power in this industry. You don't have to become a legal expert to safely navigate your way through, but it does help to know some of the basics, which will hopefully protect you and your music. You will need to invest a little in yourself as this investment could prove to be quite a return further down the line.

Copyright

If you are planning to sell your music, then everything, and I mean *everything*, must have your copyright on it. Copyright is a legal seal of ownership of a piece of work, and without it, anyone can claim that work as their own.

There are many ways to copyright your material and this can be done either very cheaply, or in some cases free. If anyone says you need to seek legal advice for this, it's simply not true. The only time you would need a solicitor or lawyer would be if someone uses your material without your consent and that you can prove without any doubt that you have ownership.

So how do we copyright?

Write down a copy of your musical work either in music form or basic notes or record it. Place it in an envelope that is signed with your name and address on the seal of the envelope. Post it to yourself by registered/recorded delivery and the time will be stamped from the post office, which will be vital in the event of copyright dispute. Importantly, DON'T open the envelope. Keep it in a safe place until such time that you need it as part of any legal proceedings.

If you are recording your song, it doesn't need to be done professionally as in this modern age we can record on a phone and then transfer it to computer for safe keeping. This is called "The Poor Man's Way". I would however suggest that if you are looking at a commercial release then do get in touch with the "Song Writers Guild".

If you live in the UK, another way to copyright is to join the Song Writers Guild, www.songwriters-guild.co.uk. *(There will be equivalent organisation in your country of origin)* For an annual subscription, you get lots of valuable information as well as a free copyright service.

If you have money to burn, then you could send your work sealed as above to a bank or solicitor who will hold it for you. They will, of course, charge you for this service.

How long does copyright last for?

In the UK, for instance, your copyright is valid for 70 years after your death where the work then passes into the public domain for anyone to use.

Protecting you as an artist

In other industries, you can become a member of a union, and this industry is no different. There are a few associations that you might be interested in joining as they offer great support and information to an artist. The first is The British Academy of Songwriters, Composers and Authors (BASCA). But probably the most important one to start with is the Musicians Union. If you are serious about your music, then I would highly recommend you join, www.musiciansunion.org.uk.

Show me the money!

OK, so how do we as the songwriter or performer get paid? Well, we need to break this down into two categories, as there are different collecting pots for a songwriter and performer.

Songwriter/composer

Around the world there are many different collection agencies that act on behalf of us songwriters. In the UK, we have the Performing Rights Society (PRS). In America, they have American Society of Composers, Authors and Publishers (ASCAP). The only way you can get paid for your music is to join one of these agencies. You will then be able to list all of your material and they collect money on your behalf. You don't need to join them all as they actually all work together. I'm a member of the PRS but most of my music is played in America, so ASCAP collects it and sends it to the PRS.

Performer

If you are a performer of someone else's composition, then you too are entitled to royalties. In the UK this is collected by the Phonographic Performance Ltd (PPL) society. This is free to join and if you have performed on a song and you didn't receive any royalties, then it might be worth finding out if you were entitled to a royalty, as payment can be backdated six years.

Has your music ever been released by a record company?

If this is the case, then you need to sign up with the Mechanical-Copyright Protection Society (MCPS). The main role of MCPS is to collect money from music users in the UK who record music into TV and radio programmes, websites, feature films, CDs, records, and so on. MCPS collects royalties by issuing licences to music users in respect of the mechanical copyright in musical works.

Details of any music used are supplied to MCPS by the licensees. This information is then matched to the MCPS databases and enables the payment of royalties to the writers and publishers of that music.

I would recommend you sign up to both the PRS and MCPS to cover all your bases.

So how much will you get?

Royalties are very complicated as there are so many factors that affect how much you will receive. Radio airplay is a good example of the difference in pay between a local and a national station. Here are a few examples of the royalties you might expect, and which are calculated by every minute your track is played on air (rates correct as of December 2019 from the PRS).

BBC Radio Newcastle (local radio)   *£0.24 per minute*

BBC Radio 2 (national radio)   *£26.03 per minute*

As you can see, if your music gets played at a local level it's not a great return, but if you get to the dizzy heights of a national station then you are going to be receiving a nice tidy return.

If you are interested to find out more about royalty fees, you must sign up as a PRS member.

BUT let me tell you, when your first royalty statement comes in, then you know you have made something of your music. My first royalty statement was for just £99.98, as you can see below, but to me it was worth so much more as it had validated all my time, effort and determination in creating music. People were actually listening and paying for MY material!

		Royalty £.p	Tax Withheld £.p
USA (BMI) Television and Cable		99.98	
	Total :	£99.98	£0.00

Music Synchronisation License

Another form of income is to offer your music under licence. A music synchronisation license, also known as a sync license, is granted by the owner /composer (you) of a particular piece of work. The license allows the licensee or purchaser the right to use the music in a visual piece, such as a movie, video game or commercial.

This type of license works very well if you produce instrumental music, which can be licensed for TV, videos, corporate and commercial use. Your fee to the licensee can be flexible but you need to be careful you don't price yourself out of the market. Generally, new artists will charge less than more established artists due to their longevity in the industry. Have a read of the Making Money from your Music chapter of this book, as sync licensing is common practice for library/production music.

Will you receive a royalty if someone purchases a license for your song?

The short answer is yes. If your music is registered with a collection agency, such as the PRS or ASCAP, then as soon as your music is played or performed anywhere, you are entitled to royalties.

Always read the small print

If your music is listed with a third-party platform, then it is worth reading the small print. Some companies may take a royalty commission from any music you license through their service. Remember that it's not called the music business for nothing. Everyone wants to profit from your artistic skill, so you must be wary about what you are getting yourself in to.

Topp tips so far!

- *Copyright everything.*

- *Join the Musicians Union and possibly the Song Writers Guild if you can afford it.*

- *Register with the PRS, PPL and MCPS.*

- *If you license your music, read the small print.*

Contracts

So, you have been approached by a record, publishing or another musical company who want to offer you some kind of a deal. First of all, gone are the days of record companies offering you lots of money in return for, let's say, a three-album deal. Nowadays, you are more likely to be offered an Extended Play (EP) or one album deal as the market moves much faster than it did in the past. The Internet has played a huge part in changing the face of the industry, making it easier for artists to self-release their music.

There isn't such a thing as a standard contract in music and they tend to be bespoke to each artist. BUT there are some important terms and trigger words to look out for. You don't have to be an expert in legal terms, but if you are not sure of the wording, don't sign anything until you have had it checked by a reputable solicitor. OR, as a Musicians Union member, they can advise you more specifically as they have your best interests at heart.

Just remember if a company offers you a contract then it's in essence giving you a loan, which you will have to pay back if you don't fulfil your commitments to them.

Let's have a look at some of the common terms and what you need to know. You will need to ask yourself the following questions:

- How much will I get?
- What will I be giving away?
- How long am I tied into the contract?
- What will I be getting from the company?
- How do I get out of the contract?

You need to be clear on what you want and why you want to sign with them. It's like going for a job interview. Yes, they are interviewing you, but you also need to be interviewing them to see if it's a right fit for your career.

Contract terms

- **Purpose**

Recording contracts are legally binding agreements, enabling record and other companies to exploit an artist's performance in a sound recording, in return for royalty payments.

Exploitation is achieved through the following avenues: physical sales, such as CD, vinyl and cassette; the public performance and broadcasting of works; and the sale of digital products such as downloads and mobile ringtones. The contract will define a record to include audio-visual devices as well as DVD and other new technologies.

- **Exclusivity**

The recording contract will usually require the artist to sign to the label exclusively. This means that they can't record for another label without permission, nor can they leave the contract if they're unhappy. The label, however, remains free to sign and promote as many artists as it wishes. Record labels invest huge sums of money in breaking an act and claim that they need this level of control in order to improve the chances of making a profit, or as is more often the case, to cut their losses. Occasionally the artist gets one over on the label.

If an artist wants to make a guest appearance on another artist's record, they'll need a 'sideman' provision to cover this. If you are a DJ or producer, you can sign deals under a specific alias, leaving you free to contract with other labels under a different pseudonym.

- **Territory**

Major labels will normally sign the artist to a worldwide deal. Companies such as Universal and Sony/BMG have offices in all the key markets, together with the vast distribution network capable of delivering their latest offerings to a music store near you. Split-territory deals are less likely with major record labels, but independents may be more willing to agree to such an arrangement.

- **Term**

Now this is quite an important section to be aware of. This relates to the duration of the contract. It is calculated by reference to an initial fixed period of maybe 12 months — when you'll make your first album — followed by further option periods, also usually of 12 months, allowing the record company to extend the contract if they wish. There will be a minimum commitment within each period, requiring you to deliver a certain number of tracks, to a releasable standard, with perhaps a total of five or six albums expected under the deal. This kind of term doesn't happen as much these days because, as we explained earlier, the industry has changed a lot over the last few years.

- **Rights Granted**

Under most exclusive recording contracts, the artist will assign copyright of the sound recordings to the record company. An assignment is a transfer of ownership for the full life of copyright. In the case of sound recordings, this will be 50 years from release. Always be aware of this as once you have signed over the copyright of your material, you might not be able to get it back easily if you don't see the contract through.

- **Release Commitment**

The artist should aim to secure a positive release commitment from the label (at least in the UK), coupled with a minimum marketing spend to support the release. Should the label fail to release your record, you should be able to terminate the deal, and/or buy back your recordings, so they can be licensed to another label, or perhaps self-released.

- **Advances**

These are sums of money paid to the artist on account of future royalties. They're paid when the artist signs to the label, and again as and when further options are exercised.

More generous advances should be negotiated for the exercise of successive options — ie. when the next album becomes due — irrespective of whether previous advances have been recouped.

- **Recoupment**

Recoupment is a process by which the label will first recover the advance against any artist royalty income. Care should be taken to remove any wording stating that an advance is repayable. This would have the effect of turning it into a personal debt, which you could be liable for at any time. You should only ever have to repay advances where your record sales generate sufficient royalties to cover them. Failing that, the label bears the loss.

Remember, you'll probably have to split your advance with your manager and other members of your band (if there are any), as well as with the taxman, who will also take his cut. So even a generous advance can be eroded quite quickly.

- **Recording Costs**

Advances are often provided as part of an inclusive recording fund. A certain amount will be allocated to the recording budget and any surplus goes into the pocket of the artist. The full amount is recoupable, so don't be tempted to go on a spending spree as you will have nothing left to live on and no record either.

You must also make sure you only allow your manager commission on the non-recording portion of the fund — specifically, what's left over after the recording budget has been agreed. This is your personal advance, on which your manager will take his 20%.

Although the thought of large advances may get you excited, they come at a price. Often, if the advance is large, there'll be more pressure on an artist to succeed immediately. If the first record is a flop, the label may cut its losses and simply 'drop' you. If you're after a little more stability and you truly believe in yourself, you should probably opt for a smaller advance and instead aim to secure a higher royalty rate.

- **Royalties**

Artists are paid royalties based on record sales. In a typical major-label deal, the artist will earn somewhere between 14 - 18% of the record's dealer price (PPD) which may be between £6.50 and £8.50.

Before they'll see any money, the artist will have to recoup the recording costs, advances, and usually 50% of all video costs. The label will make additional deductions, reducing the real royalty rate still further.

Standard deductions, or standard as far as record labels are concerned, include a packaging deduction of 20 – 25% on CDs, a reduced royalty rate on foreign sales, budget records and record clubs, a reduced royalty on TV-advertised albums, and often no royalty at all on free goods (records given away to retailers and the media). Because you only get paid on royalty-bearing records, you'll need a cap on free goods, otherwise you'll be in trouble.

Overall, you might only get paid on 90% of actual sales, since retailers are able to return records they don't sell. The record label therefore holds on to a portion of your royalties, usually 10%, as a reserve, until all sales are verified. You must make sure that this reserve will be liquidated (paid out) at regular intervals, and that the artist (you) receives their entitlement in full.

In reality, most 'deductions' are artificial and in no way reflect the true cost to the label. Packaging on CDs manufactured in volume is cheap. Similarly, as more records are sold through digital channels, a reserve for breakages and the allocation of free digital goods ceases to make any sense at all, other than to boost the label's profits.

- **Producer Royalty**

The artist is further expected to pay the producer royalty from their own royalty share. So, for example, where a producer is paid a 3% royalty and the artist 15%, the artist will end up with an actual rate before deductions of 12%. Don't forget that the artist still has to pay their manager a percentage of earnings, recoup advances and, in the case of a band, possibly split royalty income five ways. The producer, however, will be earning a healthy three percent from the very first record sold.

It's important not to allow the record company to recoup from the artist's royalty income advances paid to the producer. In the UK, producer advances are the responsibility of the label.

- **Secondary Income**

A well-negotiated deal will ensure that the artist is entitled to a 50:50 share of any secondary income earned by the label. This could be in the form of advances paid by overseas labels licensing your record, income from compilations, or sync fees that are paid when a sound recording is used in a film or TV commercial or on a computer game.

Synchronisation exposure can sometimes provide a much-needed boost, taking the artist's career to the next level. The colourful bouncing balls commercial for Sony Bravia, delicately underscored by Jose Gonzalez's *Heartbeats*, helped propel the ringtone to the top spot on the charts and increase sales of Gonzalez's album, *Veneer*. In recent times, artists including The Subways, The Dandy Warhols, Dido and '60s hippy-folk singer Vashti Bunyan — featured on T-Mobile's 'Flexible World' commercial — have also greatly benefitted from advertising and movie exposure. Other times, the effect has been more short-lived, but nonetheless lucrative. The popular 2003 advert for Lynx Pulse, featuring a man performing a spontaneous dance routine with some women in a bar, catapulted the accompanying track, *Make Luv*, to the No. 1 spot when it was re-released by Room 5 featuring Oliver Cheatham.

- **Promotion**

In order to raise the profile of a release, the artist will have to undertake some domestic and international promotional work. In the event that you don't follow in the footsteps of Sandi Thom, by webcasting your 'tour' from the comfort of your living room, the record company will deploy an army of radio, press and new media marketeers to talk up your record. The considerable cost this may incur should not be recoupable from artist royalties. After all, the record label benefits whenever the record sells, and promotion is a reasonable overhead of their business. And, of course, with a likely earnings ratio of 3:1 in the label's favour, they're going to break even a lot quicker than any artist can recoup.

- **Artist Warranties**

The artist will have to promise the label that they will perform their duties to the best of their ability, and that they are free to enter the agreement — i.e., not currently signed to another record label. More specifically, they'll have to promise to attend interviews and undertake personal appearances and all other reasonable promotional duties. Costs incurred in connection with the latter (for example, travel and accommodation) should be borne by the label.

The artist will also have to warrant that they haven't breached copyright in another person's work in making their record. The label should be notified of any uncleared samples and all session musician consents must be obtained before the label will accept the record.

- **Tour Support**

Tour support paid by the label to get the artist on the road is recoupable, so it's best to agree a limit on spend for obvious reasons.

- **Leaving Members**

In the case of a group signed to a label, usually the company will reserve the right to terminate the contract should a key member of the band decide to leave. The label may also try to obtain a clause allowing them to sign any leaving member as a solo artist — and if the group breaks up before releasing a record, but after spending their advance, they'll probably be sued for breach of contract and return of the monies they've received!

Care should be taken not to allow the label to recoup advances paid to leaving members for solo releases against the remaining members' royalties.

- **Re-recording Restrictions**

Another protection the label will ask for is a re-record restriction. This prevents the artist from re-recording their music on another label for a certain number of years following expiry of the contract. Any restriction agreed should apply for a maximum of five years following the end of the contract and should only ever cover records actually released.

- **Controlled Compositions**

If you are also a songwriter and the label is releasing your music in the USA, you'll have to deal with the thorny issue of how your mechanical royalties are paid. Essentially, mechanicals are royalties paid to songwriters when their compositions are reproduced on sound carriers for sale: CDs, vinyl, DVDs, and so on. These are quite separate from public performance royalties, which performers and composers are entitled to when their works are broadcast on radio or TV.

In the UK, the mechanical royalty rate is set as 8.5% of the dealer price on physical products and 8% of gross revenue (excluding VAT) on downloads. In the US, however, most record companies are only willing to pay 75% of the fixed statutory rate for mechanicals. There is also a limit on the number of tracks on which US labels will actually pay mechanical royalties when the artist is also the songwriter. Normally, the maximum is 10 songs per album, even though the artist may have composed, say, all 14 songs on an album. In this way, it could be said that the US labels control the compositions, as well as capping the total amount they will pay to artist/writers. The most successful acts are eventually able to negotiate a 100% rate, but it may take several hit albums before they get there.

Ultimately, the mechanical royalty issue boils down to the bargaining power of artists and the might of the North American record companies. Mechanical royalty reductions are fairly standard practice over the pond, although to the uninitiated artist it looks remarkably like daylight robbery. If you want further clarification of this matter, your publisher — who administers your song rights — will be able to help.

- **Accounting**

The artist only receives a royalty cheque once they've recouped. However, the label should still be sending royalty statements to the artist twice a year, detailing all relevant territories, tracks and earnings. For major labels, accounting normally happens 90 days following the end of the June and December periods — i.e., in September and March.

To avoid headaches of the Tupac/Biggie variety, you should make sure your accountant has the right to inspect and audit the record labels' books if they believe there's been an underpayment. Normally, you have to accept the statement if you haven't challenged it within two to three years from receipt. Having said that, if recent reports are to be believed, The Beatles are suing EMI over 'accounting irregularities' some 37 years after they split.

An audit can be time-consuming and costly — think what it's like just getting your bank to send you a duplicate statement — so try to secure a provision that the label will pay the cost of the audit, in the event that it reveals an underpayment of at least 10% of the sum owed. And of course, you'll need to be paid your money in full, plus interest. The label may resist and try to make the artist bear the audit cost. This may exceed any discrepancy in the artist's favour, and merely serves to dissuade the act from scrutinising payments too closely, unless they're confident a large sum is missing.

- **Termination**

The contract should anticipate scenarios that could give the parties the right to terminate the agreement. There should be safeguards if the label goes into liquidation, or fails to release the record, or where either side is in breach of contract.

If the record company does go into liquidation, you should be able to terminate the agreement and get the rights in your recordings back. Otherwise, your copyrights could become the property of third-party creditors fighting over the remains of the now-defunct label. A similar provision, but much harder to obtain, is to allow the artist the right of termination where the label is sold, merged or taken over. Don't forget: the label is still obliged to continuing paying the artist on all recordings sold, even after termination.

Topp Tips

- *Never sign anything you don't understand.*

- *Have a plan of your career in mind. What's right for you?*

- *Everything that looks too good probably is!*

Chapter Eight

Making Money from Your Music.

Right, so you haven't been offered a recording contract. Welcome to the world of 99% of musicians! OK, let me set this up by saying that if you are looking for an overnight success or a quick financial gain, then I suggest going into another line of work! Music is a hard industry to crack and it takes dedication, consistency and a business mind to battle through the thousands upon thousands of songwriters trying to do the same as you.

That said, it is, of course, possible to make and sustain a career as a songwriter as long as you are open to all the situations in which your music can be played and heard.

I have spent 20+ years trying to get my music out there to the masses. Along the way, I have found new openings away from the commercial world that can bring a steady income from royalties. Let's have a look at some of the conventional and non-conventional routes to where you could profit from your music.

Before we start, it's a good idea to make sure you understand copyright and how your royalties are collected. So please make sure you have had a good read of the previous chapter of the book, as that covers all those topics.

Defining your writing style

What is your music all about? Are you a pop songwriter with an eye on writing a hit or are you a composer who likes scoring music for film and TV? Or are you a riff writer i.e., someone who makes short, catchy hook themes or a traditional writer who creates music for the educated listener? Whatever your style, you need to own it. Learn from the experts in that genre.

Let's look at pop as an example. If you like a certain style or song, then find out who actually wrote it. Take *Leave Right Now*, recorded by Will Young in 2003. Will Young recorded it but didn't write it, this was written by the now famous Eg White (who? I hear you ask). Eg White, born Francis Anthony White, started life as a musician in the early 80s and worked his way up to writing songs for Adele, Joss Stone, Pink and Kylie Minogue, to name just a few. But how did he and so many others do that? Well, let's look at how we get our music out there.

Publisher route

As explained in chapter seven, Know Your Music Business, a publisher can be the answer to all your dreams. Depending on how big the publishing company is, it will have clients looking for quality music, either for the commercial music world or TV, film and even adverts. Taking pop as an example again, you must do your research to see which publishers mainly deal with pop as a main genre, see who they represent and get a feel for the types of artist they have on their books.

OK, so you might have found your niche and you are ready to send your music to a publisher. Well, the first thing you must do is buy *Songwriter's Market*, the go-to book to find where and how to submit your tracks to a chosen company.

Also, use the power of the Internet to find your contacts and join songwriter forums on social media sites to get your name around.

What is a publisher looking for?

If you have only written one amazing song and are expecting to take the world by storm, then think again. Most publishers won't even listen to you unless you have a pool of songs in your bag. It can be easier to demonstrate your value to a publishing company if you've already

113

been generating some buzz and movement on your songs. Have you had great online sales via Amazon, iTunes, and Google Play? Include those sales numbers and a list of the continents where your music is downloaded the most. Has your music been picked up for a reputable film or TV show? Have you won any recent music awards? Let the publisher know.

If they are going to invest in you and your music, then they need to see you can deliver the goods on a regular basis. If you do get a publishing deal, make sure you know what you are letting yourself in for. There has been many a high-profile case where the artist has lost out due to the terms of the original deal they signed when they first got into the industry. More information about contracts can be found in the Know Your Music Business chapter.

Library music / Production music

In our everyday life, music plays a big part of our societal culture. When you are on hold to a service provider, which can feel like forever, what do you hear? When you are in a hotel or bar, what do you hear? In a lift? When watching your favourite TV soap, what do you hear in the background? YES, music, music and more music. This type of music is called incidental music, which can help to give atmosphere to the environment it is being played in.

114

For example, if you write chilled instrumentals, your market might be suited to hotels, bars and areas that need a chilled atmosphere.

If you are into creating soundscapes, sweeps and beats, this is the industry you will make most of your income from.

Library music is big business because there is always a need for cheaper licenced songs. What do I mean by this? Well, if you have a hit song in the top 10 commercial charts, to have that tune played as incidental music will cost the user lots of money (because it's popular). So, if the user can find something similar, via a library music service, then they may only have to pay a one-off small fee to use the song.

I managed to get signed by an American publisher who provided incidental music for TV shows and films. BUT their brief to me at the start was to use well-established songs and create something similar. One artist/song I had to mimic but using my own song writing skills and style was Blink 182's *All the Small Things*. It had to sound and feel close to the original but not be like the original! What was all that about, I thought! This turned out to be a great learning curve not only for my musical skills but for my listening skills as well. It's a really good idea to try and do

115

this as a songwriter as it gets you to understand how different songs are constructed and makes for a diverse writer.

How do we get our music out there for library use? There are many companies online that you can approach to have your songs featured on their platforms. Clients looking for musical material can buy and then download. Websites like Audio Network (www.audionetwork.com/) and Artlist.io (https://artlist.io/) are a few bigger names that can be found. Both of these companies operate a submissions system whereby you can apply to have your music featured. If successful, they will take a cut of everything you sell. (Always check the small print and make sure you copyright EVERYTHING.)

There are also dedicated publishers around the world that deal exclusively in library / production music. One little tip: if you are searching for a publisher, try finding a publisher in continents such as Asia and South America as you could be a bigger fish in a smaller pond there. Everyone wants to pitch their music to markets they know. Well, I have news for you if you are serious about making some money: Asia alone has a population of more than 4.5 billion compared to America and Europe combined with about 1 billion. Remember, music is a language around the world and not just a Western culture medium.

Music for video games

Video games have become big business over the last few years with sound and graphics becoming more powerful and lifelike. Music for some video games has actually been released commercially, such as *Grand Theft Auto* which was released on vinyl. So here is another thriving market that needs music. There are publishers out there that deal in music for gaming, so again you need to do your research. Just like in the TV and film world, if you don't know what game makers need, then any music publisher you approach is going to feel like you're wasting their time. If you're sending singer-songwriter songs for *Call of Duty,* you're going to accomplish nothing.

Music for business

Another area you could tap in to is music for corporate or business. Yes, companies could use a library music provider, but you could offer bespoke music for their industry.

Through word of mouth, and as I mentioned earlier, I was asked to compose a piece of music for a baby signing company. I did my research and produced a simple piece of repetitive, catchy music using key words the company had asked me to include. One happy client and money in my bank. Not bad for a 1:30 piece.

After doing this, it made me realise that I could approach businesses to offer a completely unique product for them. Yes, they could buy off the shelf so to speak, but a lot of companies liked the fact they could have a tailored piece of music.

This brings me to a side-line but very important point: how much to charge for this! Creating music takes time and in most other industries you get paid for the hours you work. The same should apply here. If you are a Musicians Union member, you can find the appropriate rate of pay per hour for the service you are providing. Don't be afraid to give the client a figure that you feel is too high. Never undersell yourself and your skills - remember it has taken you a long time and lots of hours to perfect your ability and they are paying you because you have the skills. Oh, and always ask for a deposit up front for any musical work you do! I always ask for 50% and have never been turned down because of it. Businesses like it if you come across as a professional. If you are running your music as a hobby, then it's more than likely they will go elsewhere.

Self-release

So, you want to give it a shot in this game under your own steam? Maybe like 1000s of others you are currently doing your music on a hobby basis with either a full or part-time job to prop you up. I'm sure you have trawled the web to look for ideas as to how you get your music heard by the world, but let me explain the difference between success and failure.

Success comes from the following:

Good product – produce great quality music recorded to the highest possible standard you can afford. If your music isn't up to standard, then forget the rest. You can't polish a turd!

Consistency – make sure you have a back catalogue. Many successful artists / songwriters sometimes have 100s of songs in their armoury. Just as publishers look to see what else you have in your musical bag, your fans will want to know as well.

Business mind – running yourself as a business is SO important. If you want to make a career in the industry, then you need to think like a business owner. What are your payment terms and what are your Ts & Cs? How do you communicate with your clients? Is your product a brand or are you just a bedroom hobbyist? These are just some questions you need to think about. If you communicate via email and your email address goes something like *johnlovespies@eatmore.com*, then I would question if John is serious about what he does.

Image and branding – like it or not, your image plays an important part in your business. If you walked into a funeral parlour and were greeted by someone wearing shorts and a Hawaiian shirt, you might think again about using their services. OK. We are not just talking about your image, but the image you portray online and in life. What do you stand for and what does your music say?

Branding is also important. Let's say you have a Facebook page, Instagram and a website. Your Facebook profile picture is different to your website picture: does this show consistency? Think big, look at some of the biggest brands in the world and see how they do it. Some artists use a logo to highlight their brand and this shows consistency.

Network/perform/collaborate – seems obvious to go out and perform if you are a musician but not all us songwriters are born performers. So, you need to build links with other singers and musicians around your area. I wrote a song, which I loved, but for the life of me I couldn't sing it, so I pimped the song out to a few singers I knew and got them to sing it. Off the back of one of those singers, the song got some airplay and sales, and I got the royalties. BOOM! OK, the singer got the credit, but I got the royalties and the sense of achievement from knowing one of my songs was being played and performed.

In business, I find the best form of advertising is referrals, ideally from people who have bought or heard your music. We all know how quickly things can go viral online.

If you have all the above in place, then this will only help to build confidence and trust from your fans. We all know that if someone likes your music, the chances are they will be a fan for life!

Failure:

If you want to fail, then don't do any of the above. Simples!

OK, so you have your business head on, material ready to go and all is looking shiny and branded. Let's get things live!

On-line distribution

It's very easy now to get your music onto platforms such as iTunes, Amazon, Spotify and many more by using companies like DistroKid and TuneCore to name two. You pay a small fee and upload your songs to them. They won't take anything from your sales for the period you have signed up with them. You do need to be aware that all online platforms that feature your songs will take a cut of your sales. Each company is different but for example on iTunes UK, if you sell one song priced at £0.79, then you will receive £0.57. Not a lot, I hear you say, but if you have lots of songs available, then your chances of making a good profit become higher.

Streaming

Streaming is where the listener doesn't purchase a song but listens to it on the likes of Spotify and Apple music. Now, these types of platforms are great, and I have worked with many a new artist that has 1000s of "streams" (i.e., people have listened to their track), BUT this will not generate you much income. Unless you hit the million plus mark, your revenue will be low. Many influential artists have spoken out about this and the government is starting to address the matter. But streaming is a great way of getting your music heard by the masses, which in turn will help your profile.

Pre-release

Some distribution sites allow you to set a pre-release date for your album or tracks to go live. This is a great way of building expectation and a buzz for your pending release. It also gives you time to plan your press release and launch event to coincide with the going live date. This is common practice for mainstream artists across the world.

Once your songs are on a digital platform, you can start sharing links to your fan base. Fan base?! This goes back to what we talked about earlier - building a brand/business.

CDs and Vinyl

I'm sure you are very aware that hard copies of albums on CD are becoming less popular, but the popularity of vinyl is increasing. The cost to get vinyl printed, however, is still very high in comparison to CDs. I have worked with artists that have spent thousands on CDs, only to sell the odd hundred. So, my advice here is to buy a small run of, say, 100 to start with. You could sell or even give these away at gigs or events.

If you can afford vinyl, again I would suggest a small run as a limited edition for your hardened fans. Maybe offer them signed by you, as this adds a personal touch and makes your fan feel special.

Merchandise and monetising

For a small investment you could get some branded merchandise, like T-shirts, plectrums, stickers, etc. I certainly wouldn't go mad here as unless you are performing on a regular basis and have a following, the likelihood is that you will end up with boxes of unsold merch. If you want to offer merchandise, think about offering something different, which might appeal to your online market. For example, if you are an established song writer, you might be able to record a tutorial video showing techniques of song writing in your style, then offer it as a paid download.

Subscriptions are another way of monetising your product. It's quite easy to set up a subscription service for your website or social media account via platforms like PayPal and Chargebee, but you need to be able to offer something to your members. Think about other subscriptions that you might have taken out in the past and what you received from them. A newsletter, gift, online offers, free tracks etc.

Subscribers and GDPR

Just capturing people's email addresses can be a big driver to creating a fan base. I'm sure we have all signing up to a mailing list if we are interested in knowing more about a certain product. By doing this, we allow that particular company to send us updates on a regular basis. So, if you run your music as a business, look to see how you could add value to someone who signs up with you. A common example is an email newsletter about what's going on in your world, gigs, news, information about up-and-coming album releases, etc. If you have a social media account, then a simple "like" or "subscribe" button can be added to a page.

Just a quick note about GDPR. You may have heard of it but are not actually sure what it's all about. **General Data Protection Regulation (GDPR)** is a regulation that requires businesses to protect the personal data and privacy of EU citizens for transactions that occur within EU member states. Basically, this stops companies sending out unsolicited emails. We, the customer, has to opt into a mailing list. For example, you purchase a product online, then the company you purchased from starts sending you lots of advertising emails. Unless you specifically state you want to receive information, that company is breaking the law by sending you anything other than a receipt for the purchased product.

Website and domain name

OK, so in this era of social media do you really need a website? The answer is a big fat YES. Not everyone has a social media account, so it is important to have a landing page at least with all the information your fan needs to know how and where to get your music from. All successful artists will have a website. Again, you need to make sure that you follow the branding and image rules here, as it needs to reflect your social media and other marketing material you might have.

Websites can be created with ease nowadays, with hosting packages starting as cheap as 99p per month. BUT even before you set about designing your website, you need to get your domain name sorted. Your domain name is the web address your fans use to find your web page. The cost of most domain names is as little as £1.99, but if you are looking for a popular key word domain name, you might have to pay a premium for it. Make sure your domain name is closely related to you and your music. Mine, for example, is simply www.jefftopp.com . There aren't many of me in the world so that was an easy and cheap domain.

Keywords

Now, I'm not the most technical person in the world but I urge you to dip your toe in to the world of Search Engine Optimisation, SEO for short. If you have a website, then this is important to know. All the big search engines like Google and Yahoo have two main ways of showing you the results you search for. For example, if you were looking for a recording studio in your area, you might just type "recording studio" in to the search bar. The first couple that show up are the studios that have paid the search engine to advertise, but below them will be the organic results, not paid for by the company.

But what if we want to be more specific about what we are looking for? Maybe you are looking for a studio that offers accommodation on site so you and your band can stay over? Your search would go something like, "recording studio with accommodation and parking". Now, when the search engine gets to work it will be searching for websites that have key words like accommodation and parking as well as recording studio. I know this seems common sense, but you would be surprised how many businesses and artists don't have the right information to attract new customers or fans. So, if you are creating your website, then this is something to think about. BUT don't just list what you do and offer, as search engines are very clever. They look for websites that have cohesive sentences and paragraphs as this shows you are not randomly putting lots of keywords on your site just to drive more people your way.

Link, link and link again

Once you have all your social media, website and videos etc. sorted, you will need to make sure you link them all together. This is important for three main reasons:

1. It enables your fans/customers to get to your information quickly.
2. It always looks good to have multiple pages available and shows you mean business.
3. It will help with your organic search rating online. Search engines tend to view links as a vote of confidence for a website or social media account, which in turn will help to boost you higher up a search ranking if people are looking for you online.

Social media and fan base

When it comes to social media and building your fan base, you must define yourself and your music by identifying your niche, your tribe and your fans. You can't expect people to find you online, so you need to engage with the demographic and niche that speaks to you. For example, your music style might be geared towards the ambient / chilled instrumental market, so connecting with people who may use your music for their hobbies such as yoga, relaxation, meditations etc. is a good icebreaker to engage them. This is something that most musicians simply don't understand sufficiently, yet is a fundamental foundation in building a career, especially for the DIY musician. So, finding your niche is important.

Blog

What is a blog? Well, it's a public online space where you can share your thoughts and experiences. It can be used like a diary or journal to share personal updates or to educate others in what you have learned.

Whether you want to create your own blog or just show an interest in others, it's important to be active in this area. Find blogs that might support you and start to build rapport with the bloggers. This is a key way to spread your name when you have material being released. But don't just stick to music blogs.

Try local and specific area blogs that have music features, and then think laterally to places where your story might fit well. If you're a one-man band prog rock act who's also a builder in 'real' life, look for a site that writes about builders and pitch them your story. You're far more likely to stand out.

Creating a buzz

OK, you have your brand sorted; you have songs ready and available on all digital platforms. World domination is looming! We need to create a buzz and excitement about what you are doing. Back in the day of record company dominance, if they had a new artist, they would arrange a launch event and press release to create excitement. So, you can do the same but on a smaller scale to start with. Here are some ideas that you could pursue to create that buzz.

Launch party/event

There is nothing better than organising a party and inviting your closest friends and family. Perhaps hire a small venue or bar (doesn't have to be expensive). Inviting this type of audience should give your ego and confidence a boost, as they will naturally love and support you. If you are not a confident performer, invite one or two singers along to perform your songs. You don't actually need to perform at your launch party - you could just have your music played in the venue while you hobnob with the crowd.

Press release

Are you a celeb in your community? Even if you are not, it's worth telling your local area all about you and what you do. If you have ever picked up your town's local paper, you will notice that most articles published are pretty non-eventful. You sending a glossy press release to them will really make their day and I guarantee they will publish it, and more. It's always good to get to know your local entertainment journalist as they are always looking for new stories. If they know you are serious about your music and what you do, then they will probably keep in contact with you.

Local radio

Same as the local papers, local radio is always on the lookout for stories to feature and is an ideal platform for local up and coming artists to get their music played. BBC run their "Introducing" programme, where new artists can upload their songs to be included on the BBC Introducing playlists for either the local or national stations.

Many years ago, my business partner and I contacted a local radio station to advertise an event we were putting on. Next thing I knew, my partner Emma Burnett *(legendary singing teacher by the way)* and I were invited into the studio to firstly talk about the event and then to read the morning papers on air! That was a little crazy as neither of us had any idea what we were doing, but it turned out fine and was great adverting for our event. We certainly felt like celebrities by doing this.

Engaging with your fan base

If you have a small following on your social media, why not engage with them? Instead of posting information about what you are eating and how you are feeling in life (mentioning no names, but we all do it!), how about asking questions and starting a conversation? Get them involved with you and your music; ask them what songs of yours they like. Ask them to suggest ideas to help get your music to a new audience. Never be afraid to ask their advice - you never know who you are talking to and they might have good contacts and advice that might just be what you are looking for. BUT - and there is a but - don't be sucked into false promises. There are some nasty people out there who may be willing to exploit you and your music. Trust your judgement and remember, if it sounds too good to be true, then it probably is!

How about running a competition to win a signed CD or even a signed lyric sheet to one of your songs. Again, this is a great way of engaging with your fans.

Video

Create videos of you either playing your songs or just being creative in a writing situation. Share some of your workings on video, as this will create interactions with your fans.

While we are on the video subject, it's worth pointing out that you can get revenue from every video you post. If you use YouTube, for example, over time you can monetise your videos so that every time someone watches one, you can make a profit. If you decide that video is the way to go, bear in mind the more professional they are, the more successfully they will be. Remember that your branding and image from a business sense is very important if you want to be seen as a professional.

Crowdfunding

As explained earlier, the days of large advances from record companies to artists are long gone. So one of the main funding sources now either has to come from your personal finances or, if you have a following, your fan base.

Crowdfunding is a way of engaging and involving your fans in your world of music. There are now many online platforms out there, which make it very quick and easy for you to get going straight away. But how do you get people involved?

OK, so you are looking to record an album in a professional studio or possibly a music video. You must be specific and have a clear idea of why you need the money and what it will help you achieve. It's no good just asking for money without having an end goal. Your supporters will be more inclined to invest if they can see a tangible target at the end of the campaign.

Campaign

Your campaign is like a business plan. The most successfully funded campaigns are normally those that have a video explaining what you are trying to achieve along with good in-depth detail about how you are going to achieve this with the money that will be pledged. You may also find it useful to include the cost of each item or service you require to achieve your end result. For example, you might need recording studio time for two weeks to record your album. Get a price and show your audience. The reason this is a good idea is that most regular folk won't have a clue of the cost of this service and this may encourage them to dig a little deeper to help out. It is also important to put your financial target on your campaign, as this will give the pledger a visual goal as to the amount you need to complete your project. Don't be afraid of asking for too much as you may well be pleasantly surprised with the response you receive. If you don't ask, you don't get!

Campaign length

Most online platforms will need you to give a length of time your campaign will run for, either 30 or 60 days. The reason behind this is to give your campaign a sense of urgency and also to stop people procrastinating over pledging. The most successful campaigns are actually those that run for a shorter period. It also means you can create a buzz and excitement around it.

Pledging and rewarding

OK, so you have your campaign business plan organised, now you need to offer your potential pledgers some exciting "money can't buy" rewards. It's worth looking at other artist campaigns that are currently live to get a feel of what they offer in the way of rewards.

You may think that you don't have anything exciting to offer. You would be wrong. If you have a genuine following on social media and other avenues, then you must already offer something amazing. That would be you and your music. For most supporters, the thought of being personally associated in any way with the music of the artist they like is very exciting for them, so this is your opportunity to empower them even more. Imagine if your favourite artist was looking for a £10 pledge and, in return, they gave you a personalised single track as thanks. Would you invest? I know I would.

Pledges can be priced to fit the reward. You could offer something as simple as a free download of a new track for anyone who pledges £1, or a signed copy of the completed album for £30. Remember, this is always going to be an exclusive offer as once it's gone, it's gone.

Here are a few classic reward examples from bands and artists that have been used to good effect on campaigns in the past:

£25 – Signed album + a signed plectrum.

£50 – Signed album + limited edition T-shirt

£100 – Invite to the album launch party + signed album

£500 – Spend a day in the studio while the album is being recorded

£1500 – Have your very own private show, delivered to you at your house for friends and family + signed album

As you can see, the pledges are all money can't buy options, which really do excite fans and followers. Really have a think about what you can offer.

End result and updates

Most crowdfunding platforms will offer you fixed funding or flexible funding options.

Fixed funding is where you set the figure you are trying to achieve and if you don't meet that figure after the expiration of your campaign, you won't get any of the funding. If you do meet your funding goal, then the platform will pay out and take a small fee for using their service.

Flexible funding is where you keep everything that is pledged over the course of your campaign, even if you don't reach your target. This option, however, will see the platform take a larger fee from the money you have raised.

Normally, any money raised will be paid relatively quickly to you so you can get your project going.

Now you have funding in place, it is important to engage with and inform your pledgers what is happening with the project. Remember to keep them updated on its progress all the way through to completion as they have invested in you and your campaign. In this fast-moving social media world, you have always got to please your fans as they will quickly turn on you if they are unhappy or feel aggrieved about promises you haven't kept.

As you can see, there are many ways to generate income from your art. But the one piece of advice that was given to me many years ago was to NEVER dismiss any opportunity that comes your way. Sometimes new opportunities open up in areas you had never imagined they would have.

Song Writing and Industry Terms

A

A&R: the Artist and Repertoire division of a record label that signs new talent and finds songs for their artists.

AAA: a song form that has only verses and usually each verse ends in a refrain that includes the hook or song title.

AABA: a song form that includes three verses (A) and one bridge (B).

ABABCB: a song form that is the most popular on radio. It alternates verses (A) and choruses (B) and sometimes includes a bridge.

Admin (Administrator): the person or people that file copyrights, collect money and account for all of it for the writer. This can be a part of a publishing deal or a separate service. The admin rights on a song include the right to control the copyright, issue licenses, etc.

Advance: royalties paid in advance to a songwriter, usually by a publisher. When actual royalties come in, the writer has to pay back the advances before the contractual splits of the contract kick in.

Alliteration: repetition of consonant sounds. Example – many more moons.

Assignment of Copyright: transferring ownership of a copyright from one party to another.

B

Billboard: the music magazine whose charts are generally regarded as the most prestigious. If you have a Billboard Top 40, you've got a hit!

Blanket License: a license issued (usually by a PRO) that allows the licensee to use all of the music represented by that PRO. Usually issued to bars, restaurants, etc.

Booking Agent: the person or organisation that connects people hosting shows with talent to perform at those shows.

Bootlegging: illegally copying a copyrighted work.

C

C&W: Country and Western. An outdated term that was used to describe country music in its early days.

Catalogue: the songs written by one writer or owned by one publishing company. My catalogue is the collection of songs that I have written but can be subdivided into multiple catalogues if I assign groups of songs to different publishers.

Charts: a simplified notation method used by musicians to learn and play new compositions quickly. (See Nashville Number System below.)

Click Track: a "click" that establishes the tempo for the musicians and keeps everyone playing together.

Close Rhyme: a rhyme that is not perfect. Usually, close rhymes emphasise an exact or similar vowel sound. For instance, cat/had as opposed to the perfect rhyme, cat/bat.

Collaboration: two or more writers creating a work together. Sometimes includes a lyricist and a composer. Can also just be more than one writer creating the whole piece together.

Compulsory License: after a song is granted a first license and released commercially, a compulsory license kicks into effect. At that point, anyone can record the song, but they must still pay for its use just like the original licensee did.

Controlled Composition (Controlled Comp): many recording artists have a clause in their contracts with the record label that requires the label to only pay 50-75% of the statutory rate for any song that the artist had a hand in writing. Unbeknownst to many writers who write with an artist, this clause also affects the other writers on the song. When you write with a recording artist, you should always ask if they have a controlled comp clause in their contract. You don't have to agree to it, but not agreeing to it can harm your relationship with the artist.

Co-Pub: an agreement between a writer and a publisher that gives each of them a portion of the publishing share of a song. Beginning writers do not usually get a co-pub.

Copyright: rights granted to a creator in regard to their creative works. Writers should copyright their works with the copyright office in your country to be fully protected.

Cover: singing or recording a song already released by another artist.

Crossover: a song that gets radio play in more than one genre.

Cut: a commercially released recording of a song. Often used like. "Katy Perry cut my song!"

D

Demo: stands for "demonstration recording". A demo is a recording that is only to be used for showing or demonstrating your song for people. It is not licensable for commercial use in any way.

Discography: a list of songs that an artist has recorded or that a writer has had recorded.

E

Exclusive Rights: granting someone the sole right to use the copyrighted work.

Exclusive Song Writing Agreement: an agreement between a publisher and a writer that grants the publisher some portion of ownership of every song written by the songwriter during a specified term. Usually these agreements are one-year deals with "options". Options are extra years that the publisher can add to the agreement at their discretion. Each year, the publisher will let the writer know if they are picking up his/her option for the following year.

F

First Use: the publisher or copyright owner gets to decide who gets to record a song first. If a songwriter has no publisher, then he/she gets to decide who may record the song first.

Flat: singing a little below the correct note in a melody.

Full Pub: an agreement between a writer and a publisher that gives the publisher 100% of the publishing share on all of the songs created by the writer during a specific term.

Fly: studio talk for copying and pasting a section of a song into another section instead of singing or recording it again. For instance, a singer might sing a chorus beautifully and the engineer can copy that vocal to every chorus in the song.

H

Harry Fox Agency: collects mechanical royalties for songwriters and publishers. Also assists in granting licenses for mechanical, sync and foreign uses.

Hit: a song that makes it into the Billboard Top 40 in any genre.

Hook: a lyrical or musical piece of a song that is catchy and repetitive. The hooks in a song are generally the parts that people remember. Hook may also be used instead of the word title. The title of a song is almost always one of the hooks in the song.

Hold: when an artist, label or producer likes a song, they may put it on hold, meaning that they are asking for first right of refusal on recording that song. Usually holds are open ended, but a copyright owner may limit that hold. For example, you could say, "I will hold the song for you for two months, but at that point, you must record it, or I will pitch it to other people." A hold is an informal agreement.

I

Independent Publisher/Label: a publisher or label that is not affiliated with one of the major publishing corporations such as Sony, BMG, Universal, Warner Brothers, etc.

Indie: an independent record label, publisher or writer.

Infringement: stealing someone else's work. We all look for song ideas in the same places but taking a significant portion of someone else's melody or lyric is stealing and can get you sued. (You can't copyright titles.)

Intellectual Property: anything you create that can have commercial value.

Internal Rhyme: rhyming the middle and end of a line. Or rhyming internally within one line in some other way.

K

Key: the tonal centre or base for a song. A song in the key of C has the C note as its root.

L

Lead: usually refers to the instrument that is carrying the bulk of the weight in a recording. For instance, you could have a guitar or piano lead in a song.

Lyric:– the words to a song.

Lyricist: the person who writes words to a song. Some lyricists also write music, but others only write the words.

M

Major Publisher/Label: one of the major corporate publishers/labels including Warner Brothers, Sony, Universal and BMG.

Master: a master is the fully commercial version of a recording. When you record a master, you pay the musician's master scale, and the song can be sold or commercialised in any way you choose.

Mastering: the act of finalising a mix and compressing it so that it will sound great on the radio.

Mechanical License: the license to record and release a physical product. Can also include sheet music and other items to be sold.

Mechanical Royalties: royalties for all types of physical sales, including downloads from services like iTunes, sheet music, CDs, etc.

Melody Writer: one who writes the melody for songs. Some melody writers only write melodies and others write lyrics as well.

MIDI: musical instrument digital interface.

MP3: a compressed musical file that is small enough to be e-mailed.

Music Row: the area of Nashville, Tennessee, that includes many record labels, studios and publishing houses. Generally considered to be 16th and 17th Ave South and surrounding areas.

Mix: usually refers to the act of setting the levels, effects and EQ on a song so that every piece of the song has its own audio "space".

N

Nashville Number System: a musical notation system created in Nashville that allows musicians to quickly learn new songs and to change keys on the fly. The number one represents the tonic or root note and the other numbers just follow the scale upward. For instance, in the key of C, 1=C 2=D 3=E 4=F 5=G 6=A 7=B. Singular numbers represent major chords, and minor chords are noted as Em (E minor). In the key of G, the numbers:

I   IV   VIm   V would represent G, C, Em and D

You could use the same notation and switching to the key of D would make those same numbers represent D, G, Bm, and A.

NMPA: National Music Publishers Association, a trade organisation representing music publishers and their affiliated songwriters through lobbying and legislation reform to help publishers and writers get their fair share of music revenue.

O

Off Card: on occasion, union musicians may agree to play "off card", meaning they are not reporting the session to the union. This can get them in trouble with the union and is not the best practice to request.

Overdub: after the initial pass at a recording, a musician may want to add another part. This is called an overdub. Overdubs may occur in the same session as the original or may be added later.

P

Perfect Rhyme: rhymes like cat/bat or star/bar are perfect rhymes. They typically include the same vowel sound and the same consonant sound.

Performance Royalty: the royalties paid to writers and publishers for public performances or broadcasts of a song. Public performances would include concerts, festivals, bars, restaurants, etc. Broadcasts would include radio, TV, movies, streaming, etc. Performance royalties are collected by PROs (see below).

Pitch: to play your songs for someone so that they might record them. Song pluggers are professionals who pitch songs – sometimes for publishers and other times independently.

Plugger: someone who professionally pitches songs. Song pluggers are usually paid a monthly retainer plus bonuses when they get songs recorded.

Press Kit: a package for an artist that generally includes a headshot, bio, discography, contact, and booking information.

PRO: Performing rights organisations. In the UK, the Performing Rights Society (PRS) and the Mechanical Copyright Protection Service (MCPS) are the main royalty collection agencies. In the US, those include ASCAP, BMI, SESAC and several newly formed organisations. Canada has SOCAN. Most countries have at least one PRO to collect performance royalties.

Producer: the person in charge of recording an album for an artist. The producer manages the budget for the project as well as the actual recording and selection of songs.

Public Domain: works for which the copyright has expired are in the public domain, meaning that anyone can use them for any purpose without paying a fee to the creator of the work. Copyright usually expires 50-75 years after the death of the writer(s).

Publisher: Publishers work to develop writers and to exploit those writers' songs. The publisher usually pays the writer an advance on royalties, copyrights and licenses their works, collects royalties from all sources and pays the writer after advances have been recouped.

Q

Quota: most staff songwriters have a quota of somewhere in the region of 12 wholly written songs accepted by the publisher per year. A song written with one other person would be counted as ½ of a song towards the quota. Songwriters who do not meet their quota will not be released from their contract until they do.

R

R&B: rhythm and blues.

Recoupable: an expense that the writer or artist will have to pay back.

Recouped: publishers and record labels give writers and artists advances. They also usually front the money for demos or records to be made. When the first money from sales begins to roll in, the publishers or labels get to recoup those advances and recording costs before they split the money with the artists or writers. When the advances are paid back, the writer or artist has recouped and will be seeing more money. Recouping is a good thing!

Residual Income: money that a writer collects from a song written in the past. When you get a big hit, that residual income just keeps rolling in!

Reversion Clause: usually refers to a clause in a contract that allows the copyright to go back to the writer in the event that the publisher doesn't get the song recorded within a specified time.

Royalties: money paid to a writer for a song that is recorded, sold or performed.

S

Scratch Vocal: the vocal that is sung to guide the musicians during a tracking session. The scratch vocal is replaced later when the singer can take more time to get it right.

Self-Published: a writer who does not have a publisher is self-published.

Selling a Catalogue: if a writer has some part of their publishing (see "co-pub" above) and has a recouped catalogue, they can sell the catalogue, meaning they sell the publishing share that they own. Catalogue sales can be quite profitable. Generally, the writer does not sell their writer's share, but on occasion that does occur.

SESAC: the smaller of the three major PROs in the US.

Single Song Agreement: a contract in which a writer assigns only one song to a publisher in exchange for that publisher pitching the song and trying to get it recorded.

Staff Writer: a writer that writes exclusively for one publisher. Every song the writer writes during the contract period is contractually assigned to his/her publisher.

Streaming: services that play music over the Internet, like Spotify and Pandora.

Sub-Publisher: a publisher that is assigned to collect royalties for another publisher outside of the original publisher's territory. A US publisher might have a sub-publisher that collects royalties in Asia or Europe.

Sync Fee: money paid for a song to be used in TV, movies or commercials.

Sync License: licensing a song to be used in TV, movies or commercials.

T

Toplining: refers to the act of creating a melody and lyric to sing over a musical track.

Track Guy/Girl: someone who plays and records in a home studio, usually programming some part of the track on a computer. Track people are often self-contained "one-man bands". Because of the lower cost and difference in sounds, track people are becoming increasingly popular.

Tracking Session: the time at a studio in which a live band records a song or songs.

U

Union Scale: the rate that union musicians are paid to play on a demo or master recording. The rate paid determines the allowable uses for the recording.

Unsolicited Songs: songs that have not been requested. It is best to never drop off unsolicited songs.

V

Vocals: the voice of the song. The singer lays down a lead vocal which is the melody for the song and possibly background vocals which are the harmony parts of the song.

W

WAV File: a larger, better quality music file than an MP3.

Work for Hire: a release signed by musicians and engineers that frees the song to be pitched for commercial uses. Sync licenses almost always require a work for hire release if union musicians were used.

Writer's Round: a show that typically has three to four writers playing their songs and telling the stories behind them.

Work tape: a simple recording made during or at the end of a writing session. Usually consisting of one instrument and voice to serve as a record of the song written that day. A work tape can also be a simple music track with vocal, programmed during the writing session. Work tapes are sometimes used to pitch a song but are not finished pro demos. Often full demos are recorded later to replace the work tape.

Notation information

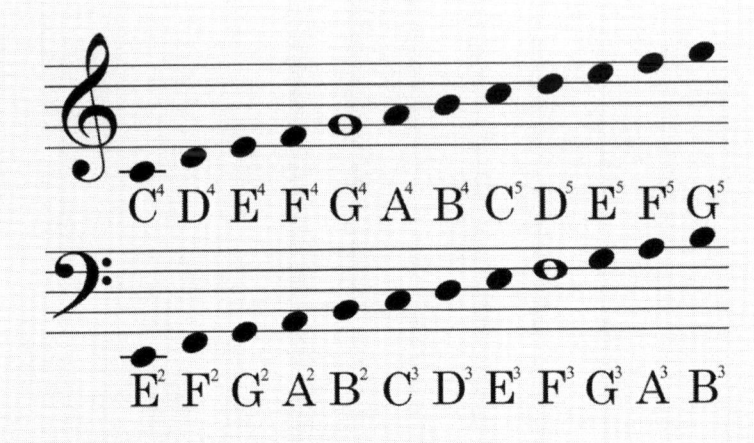

Note	Name	No of beats	Note	Name	No of beats
𝆺	Semibreve	4		Crotchet	1
	Dotted Minim	3		Dotted Quaver	3/4
	Minim	2		Quaver	1/2
	Dotted Crotchet	3/2		Semiquaver	1/4

Basic Glossary of Musical Forms

A handy guide so you can make yourself sound like you know what you are talking about.

A

Air/Ayre: (1) an English song or melody from the 16th to the 19th century; (2) a 16th century solo song with lute accompanied.

Aleatory music: music in which chance or indeterminacy are compositional elements.

Anthem: a choral setting (often with solo voice parts and organ accompaniment) of an English language religious or moral text, usually for performance during Protestant services.

Antiphon: a liturgical chant sung as the response to the verses of a psalm.

Arabesque: a short piece of music featuring various melodic, contrapuntal or harmonic decorations.

B

Bagatelle: a short, light instrumental piece of music of no specified form, usually for piano.

Ballade: (1) a 14th-15th century French song form which set poetry to music; (2) an instrumental (usually piano) piece with dramatic narrative qualities.

Bar – one measure of music on a musical score. In country music, the setting for much of the action sung about.

Barcarolle: song or instrumental piece in a swaying 6/8 time (i.e., suggesting the lilting motion of a Venetian gondola).

Berceuse: a soft instrumental piece or lullaby, usually in a moderate 6/8 tempo; a lullaby.

Bridge – a piece of the song that departs from the verse/chorus structure which has already been established musically. Often, bridges are used to tie up loose ends or to add a twist to the plot of the song.

C

Canon: a contrapuntal form in two or more (voice or instrumental) parts, in which the melody is introduced by one part and then repeated by the next before each previous part has finished (i.e., such that overlapping of parts occurs).

Cantata: term applied to a 17th-18th century multi-movement non-theatrical and non-liturgical vocal genre; subsequently used to describe large-scale vocal works in the same spirit, generally for soloists, chorus and orchestra; may also be for solo voice and accompaniment.

Canzona: (1) 16th-17th century instrumental genre in the manner of a French polyphonic chanson, characterised by the juxtaposition of short contrasting sections; (2) term applied to any of several types of secular vocal music.

Caprice/capriccio: term describing a variety of short composition types characterised by lightness, fancy, or improvisational manner.

Carol: since the 19th century, generally a song that is in four-part harmony, simple form, and having to do with the Virgin Mary or Christmas.

Chaconne: a slow, stately instrumental work in duple meter employing variations.

Chanson: French for song; in particular, a style of 14th- to 16th century French song for voice or voices, often with instrumental accompaniment.

Chant/plainchant: monophonic music used in Christian liturgical services sung in unison and in a free rhythm.

Chorus: the part of the song that is usually the most memorable and emphasises the title or hook. This is typically the part of the song that people remember and sing along with.

Concertante: (1) a term used to modify another form or genre, suggesting that all parts should be regarded as equal in status (18th century) or indicating a virtuoso first violin part (19th century); (2) a work with solo parts in the nature of, but not the form of, a concerto.

Concerto: (1) ensemble music for voice(s) and instrument(s) (17th century); (2) extended piece of music in which a solo instrument or instruments is contrasted with an orchestral ensemble (post-17th century).

Concerto grosso: orchestral form especially popular in the 17th and 18th centuries in which the contrasting lines of a smaller and a larger group of instruments are featured.

Credo: third item of the Ordinary of the Mass.

D

Divertimento/divertissement: a style of light, often occasion-specific, instrumental music arranged in several movements.

E

Etude/study: especially a piece written for purposes of practicing or displaying technique.

F

Fancy/fantas(-ia)(-ie)(-y)/phantasie: an instrumental piece in which the formal and stylistic characteristics may vary from free, improvisatory types to strictly contrapuntal; form is of secondary importance.

Fills: the accent notes played by an instrument between lyrical phrases.

Flat: (Italian bemolle for "soft ♭ ") means "lower in pitch".

Fugue: contrapuntal form in which a subject theme ("part" or "voice") is introduced and then extended and developed through some number of successive imitations.

G

Galliard: a lively court dance of Italian origin, usually in triple time.

Gigue (jig): a quick, springy dance often used as the concluding movement to 18th century instrumental suites.

I

Impromptu: a short instrumental piece of a free, casual nature suggesting improvisation.

Incidental music: music composed for atmospheric effect or to accompany the action in a predominantly spoken play; the music is not integral to the work even though it may have dramatic significance.

K

Key signature: a key signature is a pattern of accidentals (sharps or flats) at the very beginning of a staff, which represents a song's key.

L

Lied(er): German for song(s); in particular, a style of 19th century German song distinguished by the setting of texts from the literary tradition and by the elaboration of the instrumental accompaniment.

M

Madrigal: (1) a 14th century Italian style of setting secular verse for two or three unaccompanied voices; (2) a 16th-17th century contrapuntal setting of verse (usually secular) for several equally important voice parts, usually unaccompanied.

Magnificat: a setting of the Biblical hymn of the Virgin

Mary (as given in St. Luke) for use in Roman Catholic and Anglican services.

March: instrumental music in duple meter with a repeated and regular rhythm usually used to accompany military movements and processions.

Masque: an aristocratic 16th-17th century English theatre form integrating poetry, dance, music, and elaborate sets.

Mass: the principal religious service of the Catholic Church, with musical parts that either vary according to the Church calendar (the Proper) or do not (the Ordinary).

Mazurka: a moderately fast Polish country dance in triple meter in which the accent is shifted to the weak beats.

Microtonal music: music which makes use of intervals smaller than a semitone (a half step).

Middle Eight: a term often used to describe eight bars that might include a bridge or an instrumental solo. Often used after a second chorus.

Minuet: a graceful French dance of moderate 3/4 tempo often appearing as a section of extended works (especially dance suites).

Motet: (1) from circa 1400, a piece with one or more voices, often with different but related sacred or secular texts, singing over a fragment of chant in longer note-values; (2) after 1400, a polyphonic setting of a short sacred text.

N

Nocturne: a moderately slow piece, usually for piano, of dreamy, contemplative character and song-like melody.

O

Octave: jumping from middle C on a piano to the next higher C is one octave.

Ode: cantata-like musical setting of the lyric poetry form so called.

Opera: theatrically staged story set to instrumental and vocal music such that most or all of the acted parts are sung. A drama set to music and sung by singers usually in costume, with instrumental accompaniment; the music is integral and is not incidental.

Operetta: a light opera with spoken dialogue, songs, and dances.

Oratorio: originally setting of an extended religious narrative (and since ca. 1800, non-religious ones as well) for vocal soloists, chorus and orchestra, intended for concert or church performance without costumes or stage settings.

Ostinato: a short melodic, rhythmic or chordal phrase repeated continuously throughout a piece or section while other musical elements are generally changing.

P

Partita: term initially applied as a synonym for "set of variations" (17th century), then as a synonym for "suite" (ca. 1700 to present).

Passacaglia: an instrumental dance form usually in triple meter in which there are ground-bass or ostinato variations.

Pavan(e): a stately court dance in duple meter, from the 16th and 17th centuries, and remaining popular in the 17th century as an instrumental form.

Polka: an energetic Bohemian dance performed in the round in 2/4 time.

Polonaise: a stately Polish processional dance in 3/4 time.

Prelude: (1) an instrumental section or movement preceding or introducing a larger piece or group of pieces; (2) a self-contained short piece usually for piano.

Pre-Chorus: also called B Section, lift or channel. A piece that comes between the verse and the chorus. Usually, the pre-chorus lifts the melody and moves upwards toward the chorus melody without reaching the peak notes of the chorus.

Psalm: a vocal work set to text from the Book of Psalms.

Q

Quadrille: a lively, rhythmic 19th century French country couple dance that incorporates popular tunes, usually in duple meter.

R

Requiem: a musical composition honouring the dead; specially the Roman Catholic Mass for the dead, but also other commemorative pieces of analogous intent.

Rhapsody: term similar to "fantasia", applied to pieces inspired by extroverted romantic notions.

Romance: (1) a song with a simple vocal line and a simple accompaniment; especially popular in late 18th-19th century France and Italy; (2) a short instrumental piece with the lyrical character of a vocal romance.

Rondo: an instrumental form in which one section intermittently recurs between subsidiary sections and which concludes the piece.

Rubato: an expressive shaping of music that is a part of phrasing. While Rubato is often loosely taken to mean playing with expressive and rhythmic freedom, it was traditionally used specifically in the context of expression as speeding up and then slowing down the tempo.

S

Scherzo: term designating lively and usually light-hearted instrumental music; most commonly used to label the fast-tempo movement of a symphony, sonata, etc.

Serenade: a light and/or intimate piece of no specific form such as might be played in an open-air evening setting.

Sharp - dièse (from French) or diesis (from Greek), means higher in pitch.

Sinfonia: term applied in a variety of contexts in different periods, e.g., as a near synonym for instrumental canzona, prelude, overture, and symphony.

Sonata: an extended piece for instrumental soloist (with or without instrumental accompaniment), usually in several movements.

Sonatina: a short sonata, or one of modest intent; especially popular during the Classical Period.

Song cycle: a group of songs performed in an order establishing a musical continuity related to some underlying (conceptual) theme.

Suite: a set of unrelated and usually short instrumental pieces, movements or sections played as a group, and usually in a specific order.

Symphonic poem/tone poem: a descriptive orchestral piece in which the music conveys a scene or relates a story.

Symphony: an extended piece for full orchestra, usually serious in nature and in several movements.

T

Tango: an Argentinian couple dance in duple meter characterised by strong syncopation and dotted rhythms.

Te Deum: (from the Latin, "We praise Thee, O God") a lengthy hymn of praise to God in the Roman Catholic, Anglican and other Christian liturgies.

Time Signature: defines how many beats are in each measure or bar of a song.

Toccata: a piece for keyboard intended to display virtuosity.

Tonic: also called keynote. It's the first note (degree) of any diatonic (e.g., major or minor) scale.

Trio sonata: a 17th-18th century sonata for two or three melody instruments and continuo accompaniment.

V

Variations: composition form in the theme is repeated several or many times with various modifications.

Verse: typically the part of the song that sets up the chorus and tells the story.

W

Waltz: a popular ballroom dance in 3/4 time.

Acknowledgements

There are many people that have influenced me throughout my career in music, and whether they intended to or not, their support, experience and wisdom shaped my musical career. So, here we go:

My parents, without your input and support none of this would have been possible.

BIMM (Brighton Institute of Modern Music), thanks for making me not just a better player, but for giving me the understanding and opportunity in the industry.

Bands/musicians. Thanks to my many musician friends I have worked with over the years. Learning the theory is one thing, but learning from the experiences of other is priceless.

References

Many of the musical references in this book come from a collection of my own findings as well as experts within the music industry field.

If you have enjoyed this snapshot of my musical findings, then please don't stop learning. It is very easy in this modern world to obtain information but it's another carving and crafting a career that not only is enjoyable but can also be profitable. I am happy to consult on this subject, and if you wish to contact me, visit www.jefftopp.com

If you are looking to be famous, then may I suggest you look at another industry. Success in the music business comes from hard graft and determination. Anyone looking for a quick fix need not apply.

Good luck in your music career.

Printed in Great Britain
by Amazon